Port Investment and Container Shipping Markets

Roundtable Report

Please cite this publication as:
OECD/ITF (2015), *Port Investment and Container Shipping Markets*, ITF Round Tables, No. 157, OECD Publishing, Paris.
http://dx.doi.org/10.1787/9789282107850-en

ISBN 978-92-821-0784-3 (print)
ISBN 978-92-821-0785-0 (PDF)

Series: ITF Round Tables
ISSN 2074-3378 (print)
ISSN 2074-336X (online)

Photo credits: Cover © Shutterstock - Robert Mandel.

Corrigenda to OECD publications may be found on line at: *www.oecd.org/about/publishing/corrigenda.htm*.

INTERNATIONAL TRANSPORT FORUM

The International Transport Forum at the OECD is an intergovernmental organisation with 54 member countries. It acts as a strategic think tank with the objective of helping shape the transport policy agenda on a global level and ensuring that it contributes to economic growth, environmental protection, social inclusion and the preservation of human life and well-being. The International Transport Forum organises an Annual Summit of ministers along with leading representatives from industry, civil society and academia.

The International Transport Forum was created under a Declaration issued by the Council of Ministers of the ECMT (European Conference of Ministers of Transport) at its Ministerial Session in May 2006 under the legal authority of the Protocol of the ECMT, signed in Brussels on 17 October 1953, and legal instruments of the OECD.

The Members of the Forum are: Albania, Armenia, Australia, Austria, Azerbaijan, Belarus, Belgium, Bosnia and Herzegovina, Bulgaria, Canada, Chile, China (People's Republic of), Croatia, Czech Republic, Denmark, Estonia, Finland, France, Former Yugoslav Republic of Macedonia, Georgia, Germany, Greece, Hungary, Iceland, India, Ireland, Italy, Japan, Korea, Latvia, Liechtenstein, Lithuania, Luxembourg, Malta, Mexico, Republic of Moldova, Montenegro, Netherlands, New Zealand, Norway, Poland, Portugal, Romania, Russian Federation, Serbia, Slovak Republic, Slovenia, Spain, Sweden, Switzerland, Turkey, Ukraine, United Kingdom and United States.

The International Transport Forum's Research Centre gathers statistics and conducts co-operative research programmes addressing all modes of transport. Its findings are widely disseminated and support policy making in member countries as well as contributing to the Annual Summit.

Further information about the International Transport Forum is available at
www.internationaltransportforum.org

Table of contents

Tables

Figures

Executive Summary

Introduction

Large-scale port projects have big impacts on the local economy and affect the way that the regional and national economy operates, with major implications for investment in regional transport systems. Port planners make better decisions when these broad impacts are examined as part of the development of a national freight transport and logistics strategy. Private investment in port terminals is also facilitated by the certainty engendered by development of such a national freight transport and logistics strategy. Decisions to invest in new container ports need in particular to take careful account of forecasts of hinterland demand for containerized trade, the broader context of evolving maritime transport markets, competition between ports and the development of port hinterland transport infrastructure.

This report examines the issues that need to be considered before the decision to proceed to costly expansions with long-life spans and a structural influence on the economy. The report benefits from a case study of Chile, where plans for a major expansion of port capacity in the central part of the country are well advanced. Chile provides the detail for an examination of factors critical to decisions on container port investments everywhere: demand forecasts, change in liner shipping markets, hinterland transport capacity, competition between container terminals and financing of investment. The report is the synthesis of four papers covering these issues and discussions at a Roundtable meeting organised in Santiago, Chile with local stakeholders and external experts.

Supply of container terminal capacity

Chile's rapid economic development is reflected in container traffic growth and investments are underway to meet forecast demand through extensions to terminals and new concessions in the existing ports, particularly San Antonio and Valparaiso. Productivity enhancements might delay the need for investment but with San Antonio's current berth productivity already the best in South America the margin is likely to be of short duration.

The Government has examined the potential development of demand and foresees a capacity gap emerging 8 to 12 years ahead. New terminal capacity is under construction and planned under a tendering system that has been effective in promoting competition in the sector. It has also been successful in allowing the market to determine the pace of expansion and leaving demand risk with concession holders; when some concession rounds have resulted in no investors bidding, this has been taken as a signal that expansion would be premature rather than as a failure of the system. When to expand will continue to be a decision for the market but with expansion immediately adjacent to current terminals constrained by geography, a new site probably adjacent to an existing port will need to be developed.

Demand for container terminal capacity

The forecasts could, nevertheless, be improved as specialised container markets have their own dynamics and deserve close attention as they provide opportunities for growth. Demand for refrigerated containerised (reefer) cargo exports is increasing globally and particularly strongly in South America. Vessel capacity for reefers has increased correspondingly. Demand from cargo owners and shipping lines for shore-side electricity supplies for reefers is similarly increasing. Growth in this demand has been notable in Chile as its exports of fruit and seafood have tripled over the last decade. Seasonal produce like fruit is particularly vulnerable to delay from port congestion. For ports that export large quantities of seasonal produce it is also the critical driver of congestion. Capacity and reliability at peak demand periods are the relevant congestion indicators rather than average utilisation rates. Reefer cargo is using transhipment increasingly as operations in transhipment ports in the region have improved their efficiency (e.g. in Panama and Cartagena). Still, reefer trade pays a significant premium, and reefer cargo owners prefer to avoid transhipment services. This is therefore a particularly dynamic sector of the market.

The configuration of shipping networks is also an important factor in decisions about port infrastructure and port system development. Consolidation of the liner shipping market and the presence of fewer but larger shipping lines could have an impact on port calls and choice of terminal operator. Horizontal integration affects competition, even when it takes the form of cargo sharing agreements rather than formal consolidation. The impact of recent developments, including the P3 Alliance (Maersk, MSC, CMA-GGM) that accounts for 38% of the world's container fleet capacity, is as yet unclear but may affect interest in the development of terminals at a new large port.

The Panama Canal will open to larger ships in 2016, increasing the maximum limit for container ships from 5 000 to 13 000 TEU. Expansion could see large vessels operating West Coast South America—Europe trades. Accelerated development of transhipment hubs around the Canal might have an opposite effect; with shipping lines reconfiguring routes to serve South American ports through feeder services. However, 60% of Chile's cargoes are traded with Asia and therefore little affected by Panama Canal considerations and vessels of 9 000 TEU are already in service on these routes. Widening of the Panama Canal is not, therefore, expected to significantly affect Chile's maritime container transport system; rather than creating a break in trend, recent trends towards larger vessels will be reinforced.

Vessel size and port draft

One impact of the introduction of very large vessels on high volume trade lanes has been a cascade of large vessels to other routes. General overcapacity of the container fleet in the wake of the financial crisis is also tending to increase vessel size on lower volume routes as older, smaller vessels are retired to make use of newer, more productive vessels. Very large 10 000 TEU capacity, 16 m draft ships already operate on the relatively low volume North-South trades serving the east coast of South America. Major new port developments in most regions will need to be designed to be able to accept very large vessels in terms of draft, quay length, turning basins and crane reach.

With increases in vessel size, existing container terminals with draught restrictions might face a degree of obsolescence. The international standard of 12 meters draught of a decade ago is obsolete; the new post-Panamax requirement is 13.2 meters plus and many international ports consider 15 meters the minimum to offer customers. Container ports also need longer berths. Dredging capacity and adequate turning circles will become increasingly important to port access. In Chile, the current draft in Valparaíso is 12.5 meters and that of San Antonio 12.4 meters. Both ports have access to deep water with minimal dredging. Plans for new container ports at either location are based on a navigational depth of 16 m.

Terminal size and competition

Large container ports currently under development across the world typically comprise a number of 1.5 M TEU per annum capacity terminals, similar in scale to the two port developments under consideration in Chile. San Antonio would comprise four terminals of 1.5 M TEU capacity constructed in stages, totalling 6 M TEU when complete. Valparaiso would consist of two 1.5 M TEU terminals constructed in stages, totalling 3 M TEU). The terminals would be developed in phases, competing with existing terminals and each other. Roundtable participants agreed that for an anticipated long-term throughput growth to 6 million TEUs, a terminal offering 1.0-1.5 million designed capacity would be of interest to potential bidders and be efficient.

The container terminals in Chile are at present all operated by domestic companies. International terminal operators have made preliminary preparations for bidding for terminal concessions in Chile in the past but withdrawn. There may be more interest in larger terminals. Investment by one of the international liner shipping companies operating its own terminal might have the advantage anchoring liner services to a Chilean port and stimulate shore-side investment in ancillary businesses. This, however, is already happening with, for example, recent investment by Maersk and MSC in manufacturing reefers at San Antonio. Vertical integration of activities along the supply chain can yield economies of coordination, reducing costs, but can also reduce competition along the supply chain. Vertical integration combined with horizontal mergers and coordination agreements between shipping lines could affect competition significantly. Relatively thin markets like Chile, distant from powerful competition jurisdictions, are vulnerable to monopolistic behaviour, and a foreign-based monopoly has the disadvantage compared to a local monopoly of being likely to repatriate rents abroad. The effective remedy is to minimise rents through adequate horizontal competition, between terminals.

Three competing terminal operators in the region served by San Antonio and Valparaiso should be adequate and sufficient to ensure efficient prices and levels of service. The new terminals are likely to have a significant technical potential to be more efficient than the existing terminals. Ensuring competition between terminals in the new port will therefore be as important as overall levels of competition in the region if maximum benefits are to be passed on to users of the new terminals and to the economy as a whole. The size and configuration of the San Antonio project is particularly well adapted to promoting competition and economies of scale. Terminals should be opened successively. Terminals 1 and 2 should be let to different operators. When terminals 3 and 4 are concessioned the operators of 1 and 2 could be eligible to bid with a view to extending integrated operations into terminals 3 and 4 respectively. The Antitrust Authority would have to approve such extensions. In many configurations the holders of today's concessions at both ports could be eligible to bid without undermining the three operator minimum for adequate competition in the region.

Concession structure

Ports require large capital investments in infrastructure that take many years to recoup and different parts of the infrastructure have different life-spans (measured in decades for quays, centuries for breakwaters). The lumpiness of these sunk investments has led to many jurisdictions to develop systems of concessions where government funds basic infrastructure. There is, however, no universal model. In Chile, the terminal operator invests in piers and quays and port authorities are allowed to develop quay infrastructure only when the bidding process fails to deliver a concession. The assignment of responsibility for financing piers to concessions also has the advantage of countering any tendency to over-invest taxpayer resources in port infrastructure in order to compete with rival neighbouring ports. Concessioning breakwater construction jointly with a terminal concession would, however, be complicated in a new large port with more than one terminal operator. It creates risks that are difficult to price when terminals are built sequentially. Therefore, breakwater projects are commonly unbundled from terminal construction and the bidders for financing the breakwater are excluded from bidding on the terminals. For similar reasons, landlord port models elsewhere in the world generally assign investment in quay and pier construction to the port authority.

Unbundling would allow the port authority to finance the breakwater and charge terminal concessions for its use on an equal basis. Construction might be financed directly or via a separate concession. The interest in opting for direct investment would be to minimize the cost of finance. The interest in private finance would be to transfer construction risk to a company with a recent track record in construction of similar projects. A concession would also take the burden of paying for construction in the short term off the books of the Port Authority (the liability would still reside with government).

Hinterland transport strategy and infrastructure planning

Seasonal congestion is major factor in supply chain costs in Chile and as port operations are among the most efficient elements in the chain, weaknesses also lie elsewhere. They may lie in the organisation of the logistics industry itself but also in hinterland transport services. Costs are also driven by the performance of customs and sanitary inspection services. Significant economies could be achieved through organising joint customs and sanitary inspections. Customs and inspection services need to be planned from a business perspective, providing services where they are most effective – including away from ports when space limits capacity in the port – and more generally functioning as a service to exporters and importers rather than an administrative barrier. 24/7 operation might ease congestion in the seasonal peak. In other OECD countries with trade shares of GDP similar to Chile, such as New Zealand and Australia, customs services have a clear mission to facilitate trade, backed by performance indicators.

While there have been some major highway investments, rail investment has been limited. Development of a major new port, tripling container handling capacity, on the central coast of Chile will stress hinterland transport infrastructure and result in congestion unless capital investment in road and rail links keeps pace with container traffic. Supply chains currently rely heavily on road transport and port development will require a long-term vision for highway investment. Plans for a new highway to Argentina need to be taken into account as this could generate significant port transit traffic.

Rail can only realistically be expanded to serve San Antonio and a detailed assessment of the capacity for the route to take additional container traffic is needed. To be sufficient to achieve an environmentally and socially acceptable rail/road distribution of container traffic from a much larger port, significant investment in track and signalling is likely to be required. The rail network serving San Antonio is for freight but volumes are currently limited on the line by the quality of the infrastructure. There are plans to introduce passenger services on part of the line. Containers are not the only freight carried; bulk products including sulphuric acid for copper mines in central Chile consume significant capacity. A detailed appraisal of long term road and rail hinterland transport options and investment requirements is essential.

The Ministry of Transport is aware that more detailed assessment of landside transport infrastructure demand and investment requirements deep into the hinterland of the prospective new ports is needed and has begun consultations with the Ministry of Public Works to ensure the necessary capacity is developed in time.

Chapter 1

Summary of discussions

Mary R. Brooks[1]
Thanos Pallis[2]
and Stephen Perkins[3]

This paper examines the issues that need to be considered before the decision to proceed to costly container port expansions with long-life spans and a structural influence on the local and national economy. The report benefits from a case study of Chile, where plans for a major expansion of port capacity in the central part of the country are well advanced. Chile provides the detail for an examination of factors critical to decisions on container port investments everywhere: demand forecasts, change in liner shipping markets, hinterland transport capacity, competition between container terminals, and financing of investment.

1. Dalhousie University, Canada

2. University of the Aegean, Greece

3. International Transport Forum, Paris, France

Introduction

The context for container port planning

Ports around the globe are planning expansions to respond to the growth of containerised maritime trade and to the development needs of their hinterland economies. Following the dip in trade induced by the 2007-2008 financial crisis, global volumes are on the rise again (Figure 1.1), driven by growth in the emerging economies. Growth in trade will be supported by the WTO Trade Facilitation Agreement signed in Bali in December 2013 and expanding container port capacity is again a pressing issue in many locations. Inadequate container port infrastructure can be a severe logistics bottleneck and a constraint on growth. Efficiency and capacity need to increase in step with demand. At the same time port policy makers and container terminal operators have to match capacity to demand carefully to avoid costly overinvestment, a task complicated by rapid technological change in liner shipping markets with the introduction of larger vessels, rising fuel prices and restructuring through mergers and alliances.

Figure 1.1. **Monthly index of world trade**
Advanced and emerging economies (2005=100)

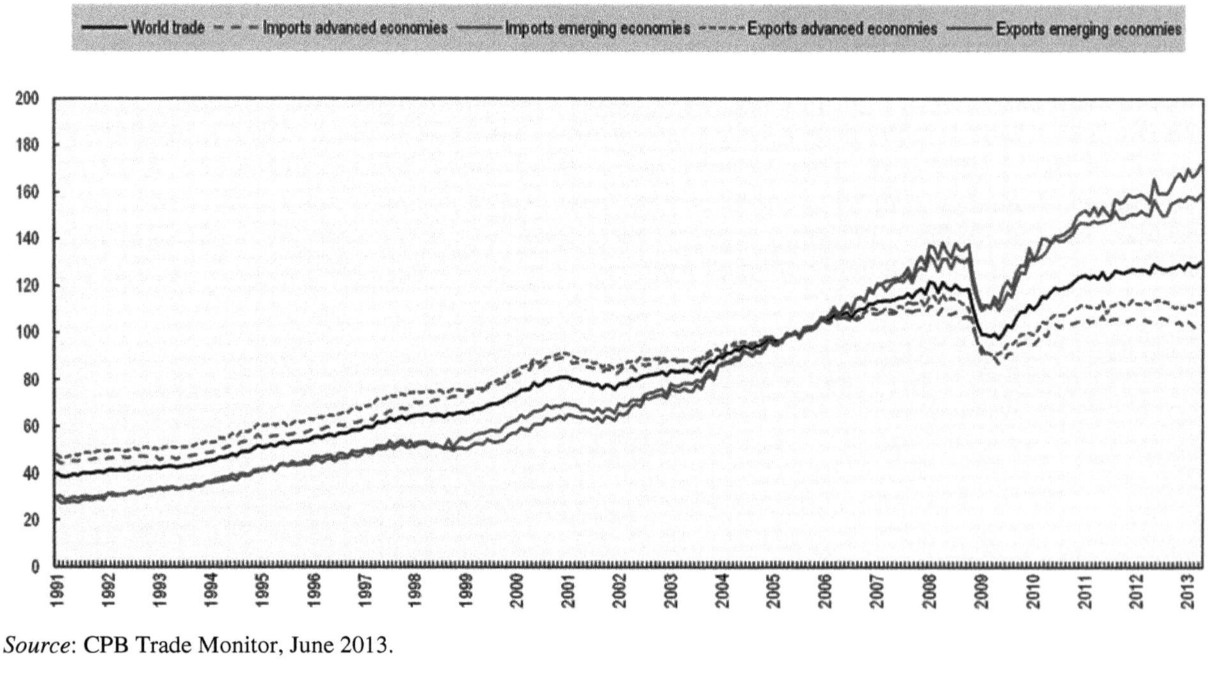

Source: CPB Trade Monitor, June 2013.

Large-scale port projects have irreversible effects on land use and multiple impacts on the local economy and local community. They affect the way that the regional and national economy operates as a whole, not just in the vicinity of the port, with major impacts on regional transport systems. Port planners make better decisions when these broad impacts are examined as part of the development of a national freight transport and logistics strategy. Private investment in port terminals is also facilitated by the certainty engendered by development of such a national freight transport and logistics strategy. Decisions to invest in new container ports need in particular to take careful account of forecasts of hinterland demand for containerized trade, the broader context of evolving maritime transport markets, competition between ports, the development of port hinterland transport infrastructure, community attitudes towards port traffic and environmental issues.

This report summarises a roundtable on Port Investment and Container Shipping Markets held in Santiago, Chile in November 2013 that examined the issues that need to be considered before the decision to proceed to costly expansions with long-life spans and a structural influence on the local and national economy. The report benefits from a case study of Chile, where plans for a major expansion of port capacity in the central part of the country are well advanced. Chile provides the detail for an examination of factors critical to decisions on container port investments everywhere:

- demand forecasts;
- change in liner shipping markets;
- hinterland transport capacity;
- competition between container terminals; and
- financing of investment.

The report is organised in 5 sections that address these issues in turn.

Case study: Chile

Geographical location and physical geography make Chile more dependent on maritime trade infrastructure than many other economies. Chile's exports account for 38% of GDP compared to an average of 27% in OECD countries. Approximately 95% of Chile's foreign trade is transferred through its ports, with 75% of the total tonnage transferred by three ports – Valparaiso, San Antonio, and San Vicente – located in the central-south part of the country, close to the centre of economic activity around Santiago and some of the country's main agricultural areas. Ports in the north and south account, respectively, for the major part of mine and forest products. Container transport is concentrated in the three central ports.

The national port system uses a landlord model of port governance, widely applied around the globe. Following reform of the national port sector in the 1990s, responsibilities for port development was devolved in 1997 to 10 autonomous local Port Authorities (Empresas Portuarias), the mandate of which is to ensure good quality infrastructure and efficient port operations whilst maintaining sound finances[1]. There are also 14 privately owned public-use ports, carrying various cargoes as well as smaller amounts of container traffic (Wilmsmeier 2013).

The Chilean landlord port model differs from that typical in Europe and North America in two ways. Terminal operators rather than port authorities are responsible for investment in piers and quays and port authorities are explicitly excluded from performing cargo handling operations. While port authorities in Chile purchase land for port development, they must concession freight transfer operations and pier infrastructure development to private operators. Sixteen years after the reform, seven out of 10 Port Authorities had concessioned at least one terminal.

Chile's rapid economic development is reflected in container traffic growth and investments are underway to meet forecast demand through extensions to terminals and new concessions in the existing ports (Figure 1.2). Whether planned investment might be delayed, and for how long, by enhancing productivity at the two terminals are questions to be considered. Additional productivity enhancements might delay the need for investment, but with San Antonio's current berth productivity already the best in South America, the delay may be of short duration.[2] With committed facilities potentially reaching saturation in a decade, a major expansion of port capacity is planned. In this context the Ministry of Transport began work on a National Ports Development Plan in 2012 to provide long-range vision on port capacity needs and a strategy for landside infrastructure development so that private investments in port terminals are able to deliver the services needed by the national economy. Following an initial examination of four potential locations in the central region – Ritoque, La Ligua, San Antonio and Valparaiso – the two latter ports were identified as potential sites for a large new container port with several terminals. Both sites might be developed in sequence. The options for expansion under consideration by the government and the process of project selection and development of a national port and freight transport development strategy are set out in an accompanying paper (Michea 2013).

Figure 1.2. **Demand and capacity: Existing and projected container terminals in the Santiago region**

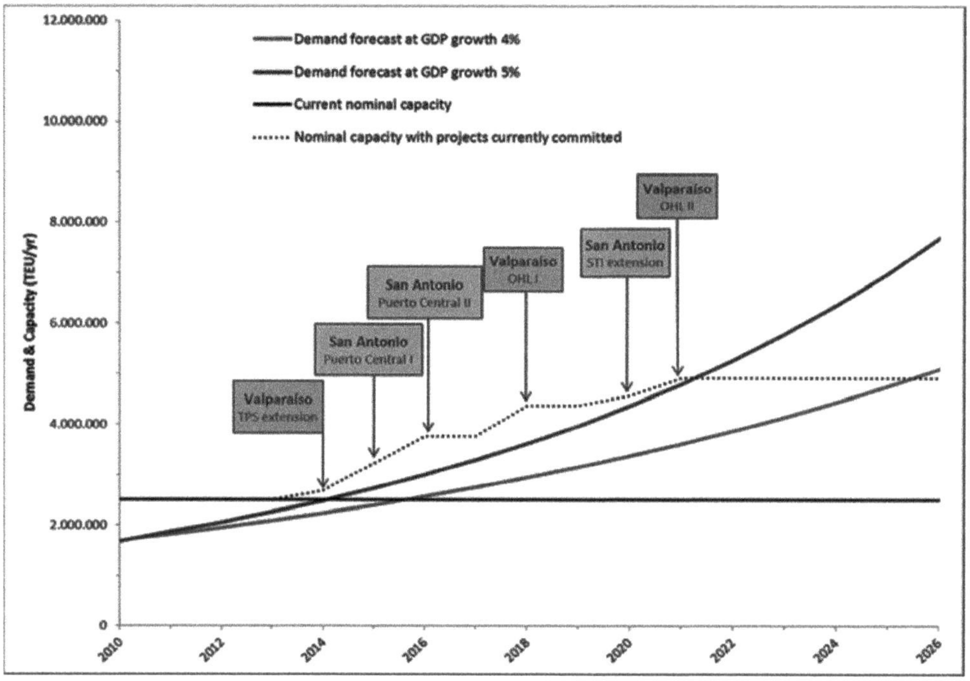

Source: Michea (2013).

In a nutshell, Chile presents a case of proactive port planning as a key to sustained economic growth. Examination of how it might proceed in establishing new capacity, via which type of projects and which aspects of shipping markets and hinterland transport and logistics are most crucial to the decision is instructive. Many countries face the need to advance major port expansions and the case of Chile offers lessons for a wider audience.

Demand for port capacity

Forecasting demand

Forecasting demand for port services to align container handling capacity with the prospects for economic development requires disaggregation of global container shipping trends from regional and local economic factors. Local drivers of container traffic can be identified to a greater level of detail. It is useful to examine port regions, incorporating capacity present in the entire region rather than focusing on capacity limits at single ports. Projections of demand need to be compared with actual, rather than designed port capacity as capacity is a function of terminal operating efficiency as well as physical dimensions. Performance measurement and monitoring is essential to making informed investment decisions. Development of port capacity and performance indicators is deficient in many parts of the world and should be given priority by all port stakeholders.

Port productivity improvements can often reduce the pressure for expansion in the short to medium term; there are numerous methods by which higher utilization can be extracted from existing facilities including relatively small investments in container yard handling equipment, investment in new business processes and information technology systems, introducing port gate arrival reservation systems, introducing financial incentives to reduce port dwell time, extending the number of gang shifts or adding cranes, and so on. The potential for such productivity improvements can be overlooked in demand projections based on past performance and future economic growth but as noted Chile's main ports appear to have little margin to improve productivity without expansion.

The prospects for terminals of any size depend on productivity and utilization rates. The existing container terminals in Chile are intensively utilized, with dense operations and high levels of productivity. In the case of Valparaiso, the operational area is 14.62 hectares with an annual yard operation rate of 58.13 k TEU/Hectare. This is achieved via a container handling productivity that averages 70 moves per hour, twice the average in 2005. Valparaiso averages 2.1 movements per container and 2.6 days dwell time, with 30 minutes average truck waiting time. The port handles approximately 1 600 TEUs per meter of quay annually; the average figure is more than 1 200 in South-East Asia, approximately 1 000 in Latin America, and less than 800 in Europe and North America (Caprile 2013). This makes Valparaiso an extremely efficient operation and the prospect of accommodating more throughput at current capacity is remote. In the 2013 Journal of Commerce port productivity exercise, San Antonio was the only port south of the Panama Canal included in the list of the 20 most productive ports in the Americas (Journal of Commence 2013). The room for improvement here is thus also comparatively limited. Accommodating more traffic in either port requires new capacity.

The difficulty of predicting future demand for ports is widely acknowledged and all long-term projections face uncertainty. Forecasts therefore need to examine alternate scenarios, at the very least to least to test different overall rates of economic and trade growth. Often more detailed, plausible scenarios can be identified to gauge the potential impact of specific risks. Producing a range of credible scenarios will identify the period over which capacity limits are likely to become critical (Figure 1.2) and can give an idea of how robust different projects and development schedules are to change.

Scenario testing tended to be ignored in the bubble economy at the turn of the century, with globalization driving trade on top of economic expansion and consequent strong sustained growth in container shipping. Linear, even exponential, growth was expected by many to continue for years. The financial crisis of 2007 and subsequent economic recession exposed the deficiencies in this mind set. This problem is not of course unique to the port sector and optimism bias in demand forecasts frequently characterises major transport infrastructure projects (ITF 2013). The lumpy nature of new port development (large units of capacity brought into service at irregular intervals) makes it particularly difficult to match capacity to demand and can result in prolonged periods of over-capacity. This is a recurrent issue in northern European ports, exacerbated by long planning and approval procedures. The opening in 2012 of a 2.7 M TEU capacity terminal in the new Jade Weser Port in Wilhelmshaven is the most recent major increase in capacity and for the moment has limited throughput (Acciaro and McKinnon, 2013). Sometimes demand never materialises. In ten years of operation the Ceres-Paragon 1 M TEU terminal in the port of Amsterdam never handled more than 0.3 M TEU and is now disused. Competition to attract traffic between port authorities that provide quays and piers with public finance may exacerbate the trend in this range.

Chile belongs more closely to the emerging economies in Figure 1.1 than the advanced economies in terms of trends in trade growth. It is experiencing rapid economic expansion and has a great deal of potential for further expansion of exports, depending on sustained growth in the economies of its trading partners. Chile has 22 trade agreements with 59 countries – among them Canada, Mexico, the United States, the European Union, China, and Japan – representing 86% of world GDP and 62% of world population. More free trade agreements are in negotiation. 93% of Chilean exports are covered by these agreements. Container traffic in the central region of Chile is forecast to outstrip port capacity as early as 2021. The diversity of Chile's markets reduces vulnerability to possible prolonged economic stagnation in Europe but calibration of trade forecasts with scenarios for economic growth in key trading partners might be a useful refinement to current forecasts.

Forecasts of demand for maritime transportation services are commonly produced with the use of econometric models based on correlations and regression analysis that often produces exponential projections. Disaggregated econometric analysis is valuable for understanding the current drivers of growth, product category by product category. It is also valuable for calibrating alternative scenarios. Clearly the potential time over which exponential growth can continue varies greatly by market and commodity. Many markets will show signs of saturation over the timeframe for project planning, with demand following an S shaped curve. In aggregate, Chilean container shipping markets are likely to be on the steep part of the curve for some time to come. Moreover, import consumption patterns could change sharply as average incomes rise with potentially large increases in imports of consumer durables and electronics. Potential limiting factors for some key commodities should nevertheless be investigated; for example, the availability of irrigation water has the potential to limit expansion of fruit production for export in the central belt of Chile. Imports and exports of non-containerised goods also need to be forecast as container terminals often share port space with bulk goods and both absorb hinterland transport capacity; in central Chile this includes significant quantities of copper plate for export and imports of milled steel.

Other variables that might determine the demand for container trade include productivity growth in the domestic economy (which has been sluggish) and transport and economic integration with neighbouring countries. Some specific developments are worth modelling, including plans for a new railway crossing the Andes from Mendoza in Argentina north of Santiago and a new highway link located about 100 km south of Santiago, which will provide a faster route through a lower pass than the existing route north of Santiago and will be less prone to closure by snow.

Specific market segments

Specialised container markets have their own dynamics and deserve close attention as they provide opportunities for growth and could compete for capacity with existing traffic. Demand for refrigerated containerised (reefer) cargo exports is increasing globally and particularly strongly in South America (Vagle 2013). Vessel capacity for reefers has increased correspondingly, with ships serving Brazilian ports holding the record for the number of plugs for refrigerated containers. Demand from cargo owners and shipping lines for shore-side reefer plugs is similarly increasing. Growth in this demand has been notable in Chile as its exports of fruit and seafood have tripled over the last decade (Wilmsmeier 2013). Seasonal produce like fruit is particularly vulnerable to delay from port congestion. For ports that export large quantities of seasonal produce it is also the critical driver of congestion. Capacity and reliability at peak demand periods are the relevant congestion indicators rather than average utilisation rates.

Reefer cargo in increasing volumes is moved using transhipment as port operations in transhipment ports in the region have significantly improved their efficiency (e.g. in Panama and Cartagena, Colombia). Still, reefer trade pays a significant premium, and reefer cargo owners prefer to avoid transhipment services.

Another issue worth exploring is the potential of demand from underdeveloped segments of the container shipping market. Expansion of the range of goods transported in containers might shift traffic from the non-container segment of the market, i.e. bulkers, to container ports. Chile's primary export of copper is not particularly suited to containers but there may be other cargoes that will benefit from container port expansion. Assessment of the scope for such modal segment shift is worthy of investigation including review of recent trends in containerisation of commodities on other trade routes.

Congestion

Commonly, congestion problems appear in ports when the average terminal utilization of a heavily used facility passes the 70% mark. This may be the result at certain times of the year of seasonality in trade flows. Extended gate opening hours can provide some response to seasonal peaks but, where this traffic represents a large part of the total volume of trade, peak demand is the relevant planning criteria. In Chile, Valparaíso and San Antonio ports already show symptoms of congestion. In 2011, a ratio of waiting time/service time of 16.8% was reported as average for the STI San Antonio and TPS Valparaiso terminals, 10% being a broad 'best practice' reference figure for the ports. Congestion could clearly become a problem before the capacity and demand curves cross in Figure 1.2, i.e. before 2021. The emergence of congestion problems has intensified the efforts of planning at both port and national level as it will have increased overall logistics costs for container trades.

The cost of congestion and resulting inefficiencies experienced at the yard and along the logistics chain differ according to type of cargo, as does the extent that increased logistics costs are associated with increased manufacturing costs. However, in all cases these costs are significant and have a vital impact on the decisions of port users. Congestion may lead cargo owners, logistics service companies or shipping companies to relocate or completely reorganize transportation activities. If Chile's central ports were to suffer chronic congestion, traffic would divert to the Concepción Region, 500 kilometres south. This would change landside costs and depending on origin/destination result in longer journeys by truck for some traffic and potentially higher costs, implying a loss in competitiveness for Chilean trade.

Port planners need to act well in advance of anticipated congestion. Due to the scale and complexity of major port developments and site-specific engineering challenges, environment permit approvals and maintenance of good port-city relations often require lengthy deliberations.

Container shipping markets

The configuration of shipping networks is an important factor in decisions about port infrastructure and port system development. One impact of the introduction of very large vessels (Figure 1.3) on high volume trade lanes has been a cascade of large vessels to other routes. General overcapacity of the container fleet in the wake of the financial crisis is also tending to increase vessel size on lower volume routes as older, smaller vessels are retired to make use of newer, more productive and fuel efficient vessels. As a result, larger ships are appearing in ports on lower volume routes. Very large 10 000 TEU capacity, 16 m draft ships already operate on the relatively low volume North-South trades serving the east coast of South America.

Figure 1.3. **Evolution of new generation container ships**

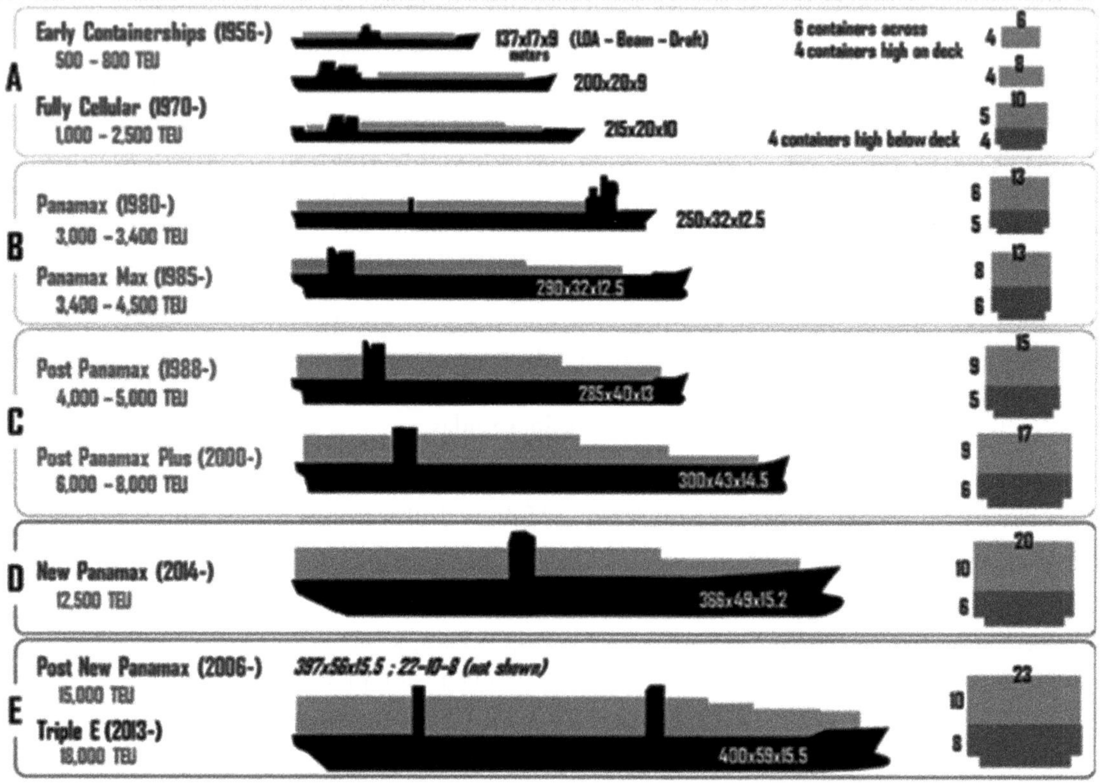

Note: All dimensions are in metres. LOA: Length overall.

Source: Ashar and Rodrigue, 2012. Copyright Dr. Jean-Paul Rodrigue, Dept. of Global Studies & Geography, Hofstra University, New York, USA.

Overcapacity and deployment patterns

There is currently overcapacity in the global container shipping market, due mainly to two factors: (1) delivery of large ships ordered before the 2007 financial crisis and (2) technological change, with the introduction of a new generation of even larger ships offering significant increases in productivity. The capacity of the top 20 carriers alone increased by 29% over the period 2010-12 (Slanderbroek 2013). The ultra-large containership, the biggest for the moment being the triple-E design, 18 000 TEU vessel has arrived. In the absence of strong growth in container volumes transported, their introduction has resulted in freight rates that are lower than experienced in the past in spite of a general recovery in seaborne trade in 2010-2012. Low freight rates, cash flow constraints imposed by banks restricting lending as they recapitalize in the wake of the financial crisis, and more expensive bunkering costs as oil prices stay high and fuel quality regulations require more use of high grade fuels[3] have all contributed to the deterioration of liner shipping company accounts and negative financial results for the sector since 2010. As a result, shipping lines revisited their strategies for vessel deployment and network configuration, restructuring routes and services.

Figure 1.4. **Evolution of vessel capacity on main trade routes and in South America** (2000-2012)

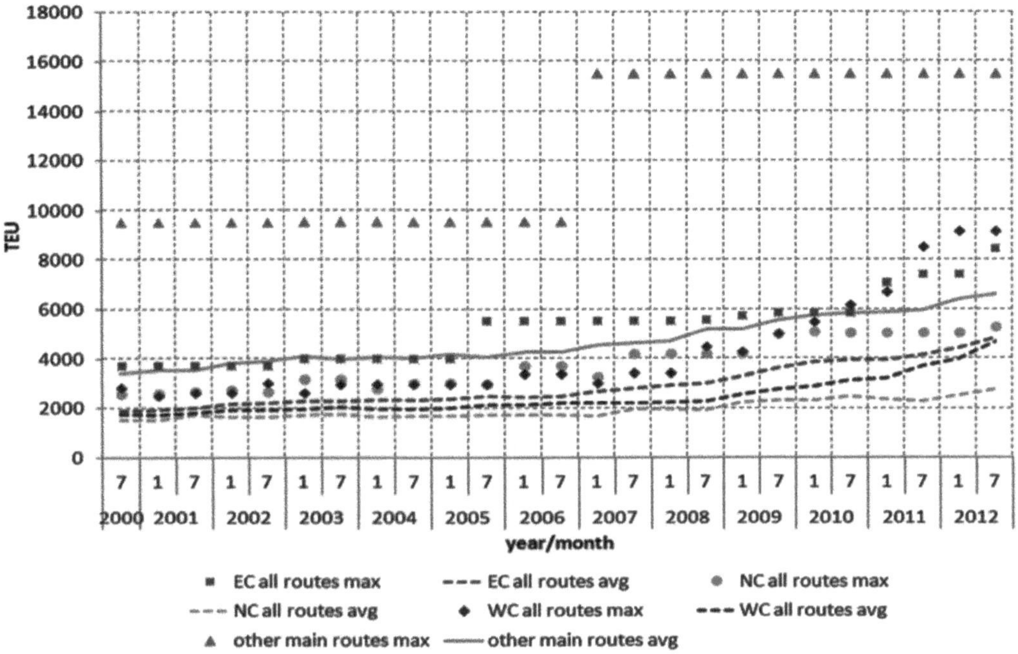

Note: main trade routes include transpacific, transatlantic and Europe-Asia.

Source: Wilmsmeier (2013).

Since 2008 there has been acceleration in the increase in the size of vessels deployed in all regions of the world (Figure 1.4). Since early 2013, ships of 18 000 TEU capacity have been introduced on the busy Asia-Europe routes, displacing post-Panamax size vessels (5 000-13 000 TEUs) onto routes operated by smaller vessels. South America is among the regions that has felt the impact of this cascading effect and has seen the deployment of larger container vessels. In recent times, the region saw vessels grow to 9 000 TEU on West Coast routes and 11 000 TEUs on routes to ports in Argentina. These bigger vessels serve a continuously increasing demand, based more on the dynamics of the Latin America and Caribbean (LAC) economies (Figure 1.5) rather than the global seaborne trade development trends (Wilmsmeier 2013).

A worldwide order book of 110 vessels of between 10 000 and 18 000 TEUs to be delivered by 2016[4] suggests that the cascade will continue. This may be a temporary phenomenon and large vessels might be redeployed to the main trade routes if growth picks up. Port policy makers need to anticipate both local and external factors that determine the size of vessels deployed on routes serving their market. In short, major new port developments in most regions will need to be designed to be able to accept very large vessels in terms of draft, quay length, turning basins and crane reach.

Figure 1.5. **Total container throughput in LAC ports** (MTEU)

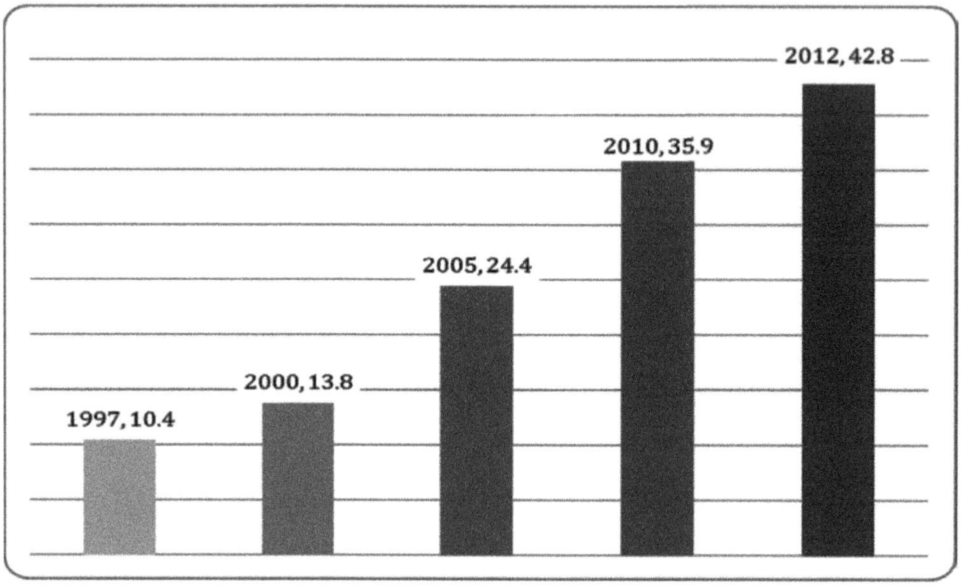

Source: Wilmsmeier (2013).

Port Draft

Due to continuing increases in vessel size, existing container terminals with draught restrictions might face a degree of obsolescence. The international standard of 12 meters draught of a decade ago is obsolete; the new post-Panamax requirement is 13.2 meters plus and many international ports consider 15 meters the minimum to offer customers. In addition to deeper waters, container ports also need longer berths. Dredging capacity and adequate turning circles will become increasingly important to port access. In Chile, the current draft in Valparaíso is 12.5 meters and that of San Antonio 12.4 meters. Both ports have access to deep water with minimal dredging. Plans for new container ports at either location are based on a navigational depth of 16 m.

Consolidation and cargo-sharing agreements

Inextricably linked with these trends is a development of a different kind, consolidation of the liner shipping market and the presence of fewer but larger shipping lines. Horizontal integration affects competition, even when it takes the form of cargo sharing agreements rather than formal consolidation.

The most recent major cargo-sharing arrangement is the P3 Alliance involving three major carriers (Maersk, MSC, and CMA-GGM) together representing 38% of the world's container fleet capacity. Together these three shipping lines operate a reported 255 vessels. The second major alliance is the G6 Alliance involving 6 carriers — Hapag-Lloyd, NYK, OOCL, Hyundai Merchant Marine, APL and MOL — that deploy 240 container ships serving 66 ports in Asia, America and Europe.[5] If cleared by competition authorities in Europe and the USA, the formation of the P3 Alliance has the potential to be a game-changer. This might happen not only because of the success of this alliance per se, but also because of its influence on how other shipping lines decide to align their strategies. This will not only have operational implications for terminal operators but will also change the balance of negotiating power between ports and carriers, as well as between carriers and shippers. For the moment, the P3 Alliance is an agreement to be implemented on the Asia-to-Europe route where its partners are estimated to command a market share of 42%. If it is successful on that route, it is likely to expand to other parts of the world, including trans-Pacific trades.

The Panama Canal

The Panama Canal is currently being expanded to allow passage of larger ships. For container ships, the newly constructed facilities are expected to accommodate vessels up to 13 000 TEU by 2016, compared with a maximum size today of approximately 5 000 TEUs. This increase in capacity to handle larger vessels is expected to significantly reduce the cost of transoceanic shipping on a per container basis. Canal expansion could see large vessels operating West Coast South America—Europe trades. Accelerated development of transhipment hubs around the Canal might have an opposite effect; with shipping lines reconfiguring routes to serve South American ports through feeder services although the volumes currently being handled on both South American coasts suggest this is unlikely to be a dominant trend. Of the cargoes transported from/to Chile, 60% are traded with Asia and therefore little affected by Panama Canal considerations. On these Asian routes vessels of 9 000 TEU are already in service (Figure 1.4). Widening of the Panama Canal is not expected to significantly affect Chile's maritime container transport system; rather than creating a break in trend, recent trends towards larger vessels will be reinforced.

Similarly for North America, a major study by the U.S. Maritime Administration of the impact of the expansion on U.S. ports concluded that, beyond the immediate ports near the Canal, which can be expected to see significant growth, the expansion will only have major effects on specific trade routes (those providing East-West services between the Far East and U.S. East and Gulf Coast ports), and particular trades (agricultural and energy exports to Asia from U.S. East Coast ports will be able to move through the Panama Canal on larger bulk vessels operating at deeper drafts than current Panamax vessels). The study foresees no significant impact on West Coast U.S. ports (US DoT 2013).

Panama Canal expansion has been accompanied by significant investment in container terminals in the regions close to the Canal as well as in the Caribbean. Development has been notable at Cartagena in Colombia as well as further afield at Lázaro Cárdenas on the Pacific coast of Mexico. Further development of container capacity in Panama is expected, particularly on the Pacific coast. The Panama container terminals principally aim to attract transhipment cargo, inter-connecting Asia–East Coast South America and Europe–West Coast South America trades and exploiting scale economies. Lázaro Cárdenas in Mexico also has the potential to become a transhipment hub, given its location on east-west routes through the Canal and the size of its hinterland market, including Mexico City, with hinterland rail services stretching as far as Kansas City.

Port Policy and Efficient Scale

The configuration of shipping networks shapes port development rather more than ports shape shipping networks. In the 1990s for example, new shipping lines entered the Latin America and Caribbean (LAC) market, one example being the arrival of MSC in 2000 followed by a number of mergers and acquisitions of shipping companies in the region. This changed the pattern of port throughput in a range of ports and the pattern continues to evolve. Nevertheless, decisions on the configuration of liner shipping networks are influenced by land-side factors including port development plans, port and terminal operator's policies towards shipping lines, hinterland size, market specifics and institutional governance issues (Wilmsmeier 2013).

Scale is important. Without the prospect of scale economies it is difficult to attract the interest of terminal operators to invest in, or even operate, a terminal. As there are no limits on the absolute size of terminals, apart from physical constraints imposed by the site, the question of terminal/port size is one of demand, competition, and efficient operation. In some circumstances there may be a choice between opting for increasing capacity via one mega-project or planning two or more separate port expansion projects. There is no standard methodology for determining the technologically efficient size of ports and the size of efficient terminal handling capacity evolves with the ships to be served. Local and international terminal operators may have different views on the size of unit required to serve the market competitively. Modelling needs to be accompanied by observation of the market and discussions with potential port users on the optimal scale of development. Large container ports currently under development across the world typically comprise a number of 1.5 M TEU per annum capacity terminals, similar in scale to the two port developments under consideration in Chile. San Antonio would comprise four terminals of 1.5 M TEU capacity constructed in stages, totalling 6 M TEU when complete. Valparaiso would consist of two 1.5 M TEU terminals constructed in stages, totalling 3 M TEU).[6] The level of intra- and inter-port competition, the specific geography of the port hinterland and the volume of the cargo base all influence decisions about inter-port competition and phasing of multi-port services. The scale at which a terminal can operate is also dependent, to some extent, on the size of the land site available for terminal development.

Evidence suggests that container terminals show a tendency towards an ever-larger scale. In Europe, the average scale of new terminals in the ports of the Rhine-Scheldt Delta increased from 0.5-1 million TEUs in the 1990s to two million TEUs and above in the second part of the 2000s. At throughputs of 300 000 TEUs per annum, it is viable for a port to commercially support two or more common user container terminals. However, the choices vary and there is no correlation between market size and number of terminals. At any specific throughput above one million TEUs, there are from one to seven terminals, but in some cases the numbers are into double-digits. The benchmarks are strongly influenced by Asian ports, where there is a tradition of providing shipping lines with their own dedicated terminals and it is rare for landlord ports to support more than four common user operators. In Europe, the maximum number of terminals is five with the median size varying from 363 000 to 683 000 TEU per annum with the exception of Rotterdam. In North America, the maximum number of terminals is eight with the median size of terminals ranging from 300 000 to 746 000 TEU. Some South American ports like Rio de Janeiro have been deliberately subdivided at relatively low throughputs. On the other hand, around 23% of the large ports with container throughput above two MTEU in 2007 and about half of the ports with a throughput level between 1.5 and 2 million TEU have only one container terminal (Kaselimi et al., 2012). Roundtable participants agreed that for an anticipated long-term throughput growth to 6 million TEUs, a terminal offering 1.0-1.5 million designed capacity would be of interest to potential bidders and be efficient. Competition is well served with three terminal operators competing for the business in the port region.

Table 1.1. **Throughput scale of container terminals in ports for a sample of 423 ports around the world in 1000 TEU - figures for 2007**

TERMINALS	AVERAGE	MEDIAN	MAX	MIN	ST. DEVIATION
1 (all ports)	320	144	5.550	1	547
1 (throughput > 150.000 TEUs)	609	400	9.269	117	988
2	1.033	299	13.550	59	2.280
3	809	566	3.154	114	795
4	687	505	2.300	153	598
5	454	507	588	312	120
6	1.613	1.066	4.000	321	1.698
7	863	901	1.194	353	331
8	1.784	1.784	3.269	299	2.100
9	928	928	1.474	381	773
10	532	287	1.079	231	474
11	375	375	375	375	
12	877	877	877	877	
Total	485	220	13550	1	1032

Source: Kaselimi et al. (2012), based on data of Containerisation International Yearbook 2009.

Vertical Integration and Port Terminal Competition

The container terminals in Chile are at present all operated by domestic companies. International terminal operators have made preliminary preparations for bidding for terminal concessions in Chile in the past but withdrawn. The roundtable discussed the potential merits of investment in Chile by one of the international liner shipping companies operating its own terminal. This might have the advantage anchoring liner services to a Chilean port and stimulate shore-side investment in ancillary businesses. This, however, is already happening with, for example, recent investment by Maersk and MSC in manufacturing reefers at San Antonio.

Vertical integration of activities along the supply chain can yield economies of coordination, reducing costs, but can also reduce competition along the supply chain. Vertical integration combined with horizontal mergers and coordination agreements between shipping lines could affect competition significantly. Competition authorities in large jurisdictions such as the European Union and USA have far reaching effects on global shipping interests and existing competition law provides adequate powers to maintain efficient markets (ITF 2010). Relatively thin markets distant from powerful competition jurisdictions, like Chile, are more vulnerable to monopolistic behaviour, and a foreign-based monopoly has the disadvantage compared to a local monopoly of being likely to repatriate rents abroad. The effective remedy is to minimise rents through adequate horizontal competition, between terminals. The view of the roundtable participants was that three competing terminal operators in the region served by San Antonio and Valparaiso are adequate and sufficient to ensure efficient prices and levels of service (Jara-Díaz, Tovar and Trujillo, 2008 and Tovar and Wall, 2012). With the establishment of larger terminals in a new port it will, however, be important to ensure that in time there are two competing terminal operators in first of the new ports, as the new terminals can be expected to enjoy economies of scale. As noted above, it is not obvious what the most efficient terminal size is. Assuming for a moment that larger yards with multiple berths do have advantages, the port project at San Antonio provides the possibility of concessioning the first and second terminals to different operators and, when terminals three and four are leased, allowing the operators of terminals one and two to compete for their adjacent units (see figure 1.7).

Cabotage and Short Sea Shipping

Transhipment is a significant part of container port expansion plans in many places. Chile, however, is located far from the main maritime shipping routes and far from zones propitious for transhipment where routes cross. Chile's ports are at the end of the line rather than at the gateway to a region of potential feeder ports. Transhipment does not therefore figure in the development plans of the country's ports. Plans for a large expansion of the port of Callao in Peru could have an impact on Chile but for similar reasons Callao is not well placed to develop transhipment. Liberalisation of cabotage in Chile could have a more significant effect, permitting efficiencies in the use of ships (reducing costs) and potentially substituting for some long distance road traffic (reducing the external costs of pollution, congestion and crashes on the roads) and increasing port activity in Chile overall.

Countries with long coastlines – Chile among them — may be able to attract cargoes to move by short sea shipping rather than roads but current regulatory barriers may restrict this potential. A tradition of protected trades limited to vessels flying the national flag exists in many nations, including in North and South America. Cabotage services represent an opportunity when considered under the prism of spare capacity on ships that could be utilised. This is particularly important if the long coastline is at the end of a pendulum service as in Chile; the liner company is more likely to drop the last port on a pendulum if a port is to be dropped from the string in a re-design of its networks. Adding cabotage traffic can make a difference to the economics of maintaining service on the last leg.

Regulatory changes may be needed to take advantage of cabotage opportunities. In the Chilean case, these were identified to be the need to expand the waiver of the condition to use Chilean-flag vessels (currently only available to up to 400 tonnes cargo per shipment) or even provide unlimited permission to transport cargo without using Chilean–flag vessels. The second option may not be politically palatable but has not been studied and so is at least worthy of investigation.

Developing short sea services is also about examining the potential of cooperation with the trucking industry. This was the backbone of developing intermodal rail service in the U.S. in the 1990s. The desire is to serve cargo owners (exporters and importers) efficiently and effectively, thereby ultimately reducing prices and the cost for the cargo to reach its final destination; exports can be grown if end-market prices are more competitive. Establishing the potential for short sea shipping to compete with road, and the efficient equilibrium between the modes in a barrier free market in Chile is a research gap to be addressed.

Hinterland strategies

Ports are an integral part of the overall transport and logistics system. For an efficient system, transport infrastructure capacity in the hinterland must be matched seamlessly to the development of ports. Port development also needs to be planned to maximise the potential for value creation in the supply chain and depends therefore on the organisation of logistics services in the hinterland. Planning for port expansion needs to take a logistics business perspective in determining the optimal development of terminals, customs and inspection, vehicle management, warehousing and other landside capacities. Fostering the establishment of networks of logistics activities at the landside of the port can create value for the port itself. The reach of the port, and its competitiveness with other ports in its range, is determined largely by the quality of its connections with road, rail and, where they exist, inland waterway networks.

Large-scale port projects require particularly careful planning of landside connections. A core element is assessment of the options associated with each mode of landside transportation and the development of a strategy for optimal integration with each mode, given the constraints of physical and economic geography and the regulatory environment for road and rail transport. Responsibilities for investment and regulation vary by jurisdiction. Port authorities usually provide essential coordination of access to essential facilities, either providing rail access to terminals in the port or brokering equitable access agreements to infrastructure owned by one of the stakeholders. Port authorities in a few locations, for example Rotterdam, play a major, pro-active role in developing seamless hinterland transport, making joint investments in hinterland infrastructure and promoting effective use of all modes available through conditions negotiated in concession agreements (De Langen 2008). The role of the central government in investment in hinterland transport links also varies by jurisdiction but even where infrastructure is privately owned, grants or other forms of financial support (loans, bond guarantees) are often available for capital investment to upgrade infrastructure as ports expand (Acciaro and McKinnon 2013). Designating land for adequate hinterland transport infrastructure is fundamental to planning for new port development. This has to be done well upstream of investment in order to avoid speculative land acquisition complicating the process of infrastructure development and increasing its cost.

Logistics costs in key sectors of the Chilean economy have reached 19-20% of the total costs when one would expect such costs not to exceed 8-9% (Guasch 2011). Seasonal congestion is one factor, as noted above, but as port operations are among the most efficient elements of the supply chain in Chile, weaknesses also lie elsewhere. They may lie in the organisation of the logistics industry itself; but also in hinterland transport services. While there have been some major highway investments, rail investment has been limited.

Costs may also be driven by the performance of customs and sanitary inspection services. Significant economies could be achieved through organising joint customs and sanitary inspections. Performance indicators would be useful for reducing costs. The quality and capacity of customs and inspection services is integral to trade performance and needs to be planned from a business perspective, providing services where they are most effective – including away from ports when space limits capacity in the port – and more generally functioning as a service to exporters and importers rather than an administrative barrier. 24/7 operation might ease congestion in the seasonal peak.

In other OECD countries with trade shares of GDP similar to Chile, such as New Zealand and Australia, customs services have a clear mission to facilitate trade, backed by performance indicators. More than 20 aspects of service quality are monitored in Australia, for example, with performance against headline targets published regularly (table 1.2).

Table 1.2. **Performance against trade facilitation targets in 2010–11, for the Australian Customs and Border Protection Service**

Key performance indicators	Target*	Actual
Availability of electronic cargo systems to Customs and Border Protection clients (excluding scheduled outages)	99.7%	99.7%
Proportion of electronically lodged cargo documents where a response message is transmitted within five minutes	98%	97.9%

Source: Australian Customs and Border Protection Service, Annual Report 2010-11.

Road

The truck is usually the least expensive means of reaching destinations close to the port and its flexibility in terms of frequency and providing last mile access makes it the principal mode of transport in many markets. The major negative impacts of truck traffic are road congestion and pollutant emissions. Both can become a constraint on port development. Santiago has a major air pollution problem with recurrent episodes of particulate and NOx levels exceeding air quality standards during periods of winter temperature inversions. Port expansion is largely frozen in Los Angeles/Long Beach, for example, until levels of particulate pollution from trucks are significantly reduced and air quality improves in the city because of the risk to health from pollution and the perceived contribution of port activity to the problem (Giuliano and O'Brien 2009). Port city residents are almost always unhappy with the growth in road transport that port expansion produces, and naturally become vocal if landside investment and traffic management does not keep pace with port expansion.

Managing road connections starts with the organisation of trucks at the terminal gate. Different options exist, including replacing the traditional first-come-first-served system, where trucks are served and containers are loaded as they become available, with an appointment system for loading and unloading. This is widely used on both sides of the Atlantic. An alternative is the 'window' system, with pre-determined slots established when trucks are allowed to collect/deliver cargo, used in some Chinese ports. The applicability of each option will depend on local factors, such as the regularity of containerships arrivals and the location and reliability of customs and sanitary inspections.

Appointment systems (even the simplest, one day advanced notification systems) provide significant benefits on the port side of the gate, allowing containers to be marshalled in advance into small lots for rapid handling at collection. They provide for load spreading, reducing peak traffic and making use of off-peak periods to sort containers. On the other side of the gate they also have the potential for reducing peak traffic and cutting truck waiting times. The benefits can be substantial but there can be additional costs for trucking companies. If windows are tight and inflexible, more trucks or drivers will be required to guarantee availability.

The near universal availability of mobile phones makes it possible to provide a great deal of flexibility for ports with suitable gate management IT systems, minimising the costs imposed on trucking. In the case of Southampton container port, for example, appointments can be amended or rescheduled up to 15 minutes before pick up, with (modest) penalties applied for missing appointments only when this limit is passed (Davies 2009). All port gate management systems require adequate parking and waiting areas on routes approaching the port.

Innovative gate management systems are driven by necessity. In Southampton very little land-side space is available because of the location in a heavily urbanised area. Rapid growth in container traffic in the early years of the century created severe yard congestion that prompted introduction first of an optional appointments system, with limited success, then a mandatory but highly flexible system that has worked well. The Los Angeles Pier Pass system provides for extended gate opening in a similarly constrained environment (Giuliano 2009).

The site of Valparaiso container port is even more constrained geographically, at the foot of a steep hill and adjacent to a UNESCO World Heritage site. The response has been to move customs and inspection to a location 5 km from the port, where parking space is available, with a new link road providing direct access to the port and to the Santiago highway. Trucks are dispatched from the parking area to the port when containers are ready for collection. San Antonio port experienced a number of severe congestion episodes on the approach roads to the port in recent years, and in response invested in off road parking areas and a traffic monitoring and alert system, in cooperation with the highway concession and police force, to prevent repeat incidents. Development of a large new container port/terminal in either city will require investment in high capacity link roads and capacity enhancements to the national road network. Freight transport demand forecasts for the ports need to be coordinated with highway traffic forecasts and the demand and revenue projections of the highway concessions as discussed in Section 2 above. Capital investments to increase the capacity and reliability of connecting highways will be essential to ensuring that port investments achieve their expected financial returns.

Rail

Rail connectivity is often of strategic importance to potential new port terminals. Opportunities for rail transport are to a large extent subsidiary to historical development of the national rail system and to national policy towards rail freight. The economic geography of the USA, for example, with a large integrated market and widely spaced industrial centres, favours rail transport and deregulation of the railways in 1980 reversed a long term decline in the share of freight carried and restored profitability. Trucks are the preferred mode of transporting containerized goods inland from US ports for routes of less than 750 km[7] but rail has traditionally carried a relatively high share of US commodities flowing outward. On long distance trunk routes in both Canada and the US rail is dominant.

The national rail system in Chile has more in common with rail in Great Britain than the USA (although rail carries much larger volumes of passengers in the UK than Chile and, if mine railways are excluded a larger share of freight traffic). Both UK and Chilean freight rail systems were privatised and vertically separated in the 1990s and in both systems passenger trains take priority over freight on the general-purpose network. In both, infrastructure is owned and managed separately from freight train operations (Thompson and Kohon 2012).

In Chile the rail freight task was 4 billion t-km in 2011. The domestic freight transport market in 2009 (in tons) was split 3% rail, 84% road and 13% coastal shipping (EU 2010). In Great Britain rail carries 9% of freight t-kms (21 billion t-km in 2011), road 60% and short sea shipping 26% (UK DfT 2011).

Containers account for only a third of the rail freight in the UK nevertheless, rail provides good access from the country's main ports to key centres of population and industry and 25% of containers entering the country are carried by rail[8]. At the two main container ports, Felixstowe and Southampton, rail accounts for 20 to 30% of inland container transport (GHK and Royal Haskoning, 2008). The share has grown over the last decade in response to congestion on the roads, investment by train operators and infrastructure capacity enhancements supported by capital grants from government.

In Great Britain rail freight pays track access charges on the basis of avoidable costs. These usually cover only wear and tear and operational management costs. They do not currently reflect capital investment costs as freight is rarely the prime user of rail tracks in the UK, although the rail regulator is considering introducing contributions to capital investment costs for some categories of freight as volumes grow on some routes. Capital investment therefore can be a barrier to expanding rail freight service to ports, although in recent years containerized rail freight services have benefited from the enlargement of the loading gauge on strategic routes to the main deep-sea ports of Southampton and Felixstowe, permitting the movement of 9'6" boxes. The Southampton link was jointly funded by government and industry. The largest share of funding was provided by the Department for Transport (£43m). Other contributors included Associated British Ports, the South East England Development Agency and the European Regional Development Fund. In the year following gauge enhancement on the line from Southampton to the West Coast Main Line, the main spinal rail route in the UK, rail's share of container movements to / from this port rose from 29% to 36% (Freightliner, 2013). The gauge enhancement to Felixstowe was financed out of the Department for Transport's Transport Innovation Fund.

In competing with more flexible road transport, rail has to overcome the "double lift penalty" involved in transferring containers to trucks for final delivery. The labour and fuel economy advantages of rail overcome this penalty beyond distances of around 350km in UK conditions; the competitiveness of rail is determined by factors including maximum train capacity/length, loading gauge (single stack in the UK), infrastructure charges (only avoidable costs are charged in the UK) and road congestion. The major plus of rail is the potential of transporting larger volumes of containers in a more reliable (depending on rail network quality, freight train priority, management quality and labour relations etc.) and environmentally-friendly way and without impinging on the car-driving public.

Stakeholder coordination is critical to policies to prioritise rail transport. Hamburg port has achieved a modal split of 30% for rail in a system with 92 different railway operators moving more than 230 freight trains per day. 36% of container transport was carried on rail in 2010 and the share is planned to exceed 40% by 2025 (HPA 2012). The main terminal operator, HHLA, is one of the few terminal operators that runs its own trains and accounts for a large share of rail carriage. The port authority ensures train operators serving terminals have equitable access to track infrastructure.

Voluntary agreements for sharing essential facilities are widespread in both Europe and North America (partly because regulatory intervention would risk discouraging investment). As noted in ITF (2009), the Port Authority of Antwerp brokered a large reduction in SNCB's prices for locomotives hauling trains within the port in 2008; SNCB, the incumbent national train operator, was the only company with locomotives authorised to run on the intra-port network. In Rotterdam a neutral company, Rail Feeder, was created at the instigation of the Port Authority in 2008 and now runs 80% of intra port rail operations with published tariffs following several years of complaints that the incumbent national infrastructure manager was unable to offer slots to new entrants. These coordination efforts have raised rail shares in Antwerp and Rotterdam although road and inland waterways dominate hinterland traffic (both ports are located at the mouths of large rivers connected to extensive canal networks). (ITF 2008). In Rotterdam 57% of container throughput was carried by road in 2008, 30% by inland waterways and 13% by rail. Target shares for 2035 are inland waterway 45%, road 35% and rail 20% (OECD 2010).

Northern European ports achieve these relatively high rail modal shares despite an unfavourable economic and political geography that makes European railways very different from US freight railways: short average distances for hinterland carriage and fragmented railway operations, both the result of the relatively recent integration of Europe into a single market. National boundaries leave a legacy of railways with small markets, poor technical interoperability and different charging systems and uneven regulatory environments. Like Great Britain, railways in Belgium and the Netherlands are vertically separated and freight trains are charged only the avoidable costs they impose on the network, usually only marginal costs. This has the advantage of keeping tariffs low but is a disincentive for investment. Governments therefore make capital grants where policy seeks to shift trucks from road to rail.

Reconciling modal shift policies with financial sustainability for rail and sustainable fiscal policy (containing accumulation of public rail debt) is not always easy. This is illustrated by the Dutch government's 4.7 billion investment in the Betuwe rail freight line opened in 2007 to link the port of Rotterdam with key industrial markets in Germany. The government was unable to attract private investment in the line (Koppenjan 2007), costs escalated and traffic has proved to be much lower than forecast despite charging only marginal costs for use of the line. The Dutch rail regulator determines the charges for using national infrastructure following principles set out by law requiring them to cover, inter alia, the marginal costs of track wear. Heavy trains hauled by powerful locomotives pay the highest charges as they account for the largest part of maintenance and renewal costs (Figure 1.6). Steel mills in the hinterland were one of the industries the Betuwe line was designed to serve but were unable to pay the infrastructure charges prescribed. Lowering the charges would have rapidly "bankrupted" the line. In the end the government felt obliged to provide operating subsidies to close the gap.

Figure 1.6. **Rail infrastructure use charges in Europe**

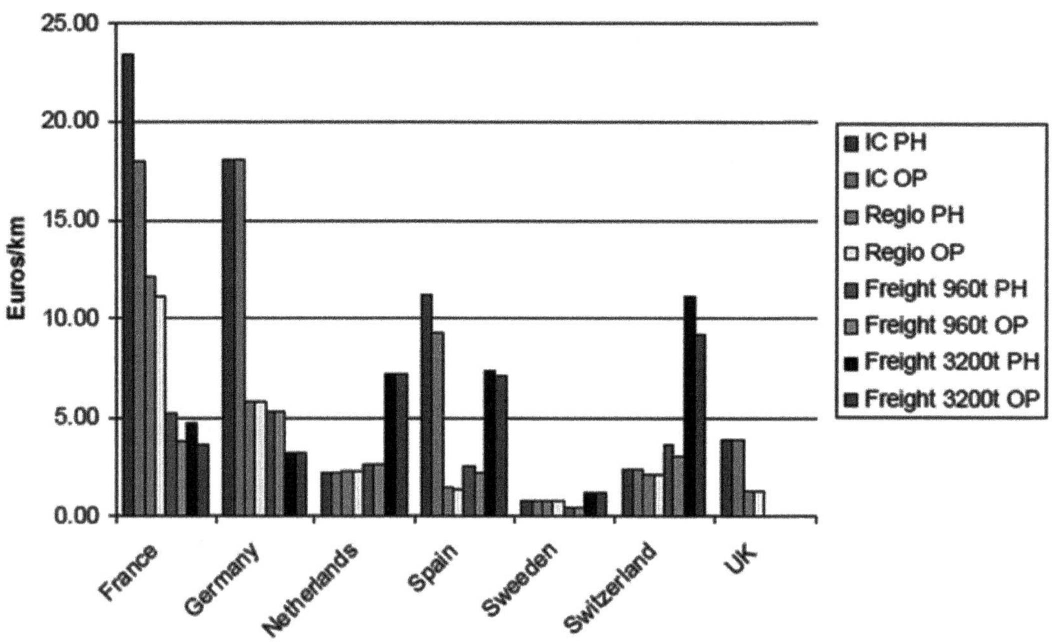

Note: For each country, the two columns to the left indicate high speed train charges (IC PH and IC OP), the central bars are for conventional passenger trains and the bars to the right are for freight.

Source : Vidaud M. & de Tilière G., 2010.

The Rotterdam Port authority also promotes rail development through specific modal split targets included in concession agreements, for example in the case of the Masvlaaakte II terminals (De Langen 2009). Rotterdam is Europe's biggest port and it is not clear that all port authorities have the power to copy it. Such requirements might eliminate bidders from concessions opened for terminals in smaller ports. It also remains to be demonstrated that the modal split clause will be enforced.

In more favourable circumstances, rail operations are an area where private investment can be attracted to bid for concessions, and there is a solid literature on rail development by private interests (Resor and Laird 2013). One example is the Bombay Jawaharlal Port project where 30% of the 4.5 M TEU transported travel by rail following development of a dedicated freight corridor part financed with equity from users that allows double stacking and thus the transportation of 300 TEUs per train. "Favourable circumstances" in India include grossly inadequate road capacity. Nevertheless, national policies that cross subsidise passenger traffic with freight profits make it difficult to attract private investment away from the dedicated freight corridors. There have, nevertheless, been a few public private partnerships where industrial plants close to ports have financed dedicated rail access.

At the roundtable, there was considerable discussion about the need for detailed assessment of the capacity for the rail route to San Antonio to take additional container traffic. To be sufficient to achieve an environmentally and socially acceptable rail/road distribution of container traffic from a much larger port, significant investment in track and signalling is likely to be required. The rail network serving San Antonio is for freight but volumes are currently limited on the line by the quality of the infrastructure. There are plans to introduce passenger services on part of the line. Containers are not the only freight carried; bulk products including sulphuric acid for copper mines in central Chile consume significant capacity. A detailed appraisal of long term road and rail hinterland transport options and investment requirements is essential. Appraisal should include the potential to carry double-stacked containers, subject to the constraints of tunnel gauges. At Valparaiso, expansion of rail freight is almost impossible as the tracks are shared with the local metro/suburban train system. The existing rail link was converted to largely metropolitan passenger train use with an upgrade of the line that enclosed it in a tunnel with limited loading gauge. Major rail investment would appear necessary to serve a large new port development. Broad appraisal of hinterland transport options and impacts is essential.

Dry ports (inland ports)

Dry ports (inland ports) and extended gateways are being developed in many parts of the world in response to land-side port capacity constraints. As noted, Valparaiso has already developed a short range extended gateway with relocation of custom and sanitary inspection and a truck holding facility 5 km from the port. The 'ZEAL' project was developed to overcome capacity shortage in the port terminal and resulted in an increase in productivity of 20%.

In Spain, the dry port of Madrid (Coslada) and Terminal Marítima de Zaragoza have extended the gateways of the major container ports of Barcelona, Valencia, Bilbao and Algeciras (Monios 2011). In France, the inland Port of Lyon, a partnership initiated between the port of Marseille and the river port Edouard Herriot in Lyon provides handling, storage, packing, and inland transportation leasing and repair of containers, having a throughput of over 100 000 TEUs per year. European Container Terminals (ECT), the main terminal operator in the port of Rotterdam and a subsidiary of Hutchinson Port Holdings (HPH), has been actively involved in the setting up of Venlo in the Netherlands, Duisburg in Germany and Willebroek in Belgium all served by rail, to mitigate truck volumes creating congestion issues (Wilmsmeier et al. 2013). In North America, there are many inland port examples. One example, the Savannah Port Authority Industrial Park (SPAIP), is a site specializing in satellite activities removing pressures from the container terminals of the dynamic port of Savannah, such as container and chassis storage and repair. About 10 km from the port terminals are two large logistics zones owned, like the port, by Georgia Port Authority. The Virginia Inland Port is served primarily by rail from the Hampton Roads port 350 km away and provides customs services, reloading and cross docking services. BNSF Logistics Park Chicago is another; it is a major inland port 60 km southwest of Chicago linked by transcontinental rail to various ports, including Los Angeles/Long Beach to the Chicago hub (Rodrigue et al., 2010).

The dry port is a cargo consolidation centre located away from the seaport but serving the cargo transported through it, providing sufficient economies of traffic density for viable shuttle services. As well as providing the space needed for land-side port processing tasks, it embeds the port more effectively in the supply chain, providing dedicated space for the development of integrated warehousing and distribution centres and ancillary value adding services. Location is important; proximity to major centres of demand is an advantage and siting at nodes in transport networks suited to extension or development of Greenfield logistic centres essential. Coordination of container movements needs to be managed in the same way as at the port, with integrated information exchanges. Customs and sanitary inspections need to be transferred to the dry port or greatly simplified administrative and customs procedures introduced. There might be potential for establishing a dry port and logistics centre in the vicinity of Santiago, connected to the new port by rail.

Strategic Issues

Development of a major new port, tripling container handling capacity, on the central coast of Chile will stress hinterland transport infrastructure and result in congestion unless capital investment in road and rail links keeps pace with container traffic. Supply chains currently rely heavily on road transport and port development will require a long-term vision for highway investment. Plans for a new highway to Argentina need to be taken into account as this could generate significant port transit traffic. Trade facilitation measures could further increase traffic, such as joint customs and sanitary inspection at the border (single inspects by joint teams from both countries; also single inspections covering both customs and sanitary dimensions). Bilateral agreements to allow back-hauls can at the same time facilitate trade and reduce traffic and congestion.

Certain steps can be taken to counter potential hinterland congestion problems. Performance monitoring on the highways and railways will identify where bottlenecks develop. Cargo origins and destinations should be identified as a basis for planning development of the transport system. A strategic approach, covering road, rail and short sea shipping, should be taken rather than ad hoc responses to demand, and mechanisms for coordinating investments with other industrial policy initiatives are valuable. These include transport impact assessment as part of planning procedures for commercial and industrial development and mobility plans for large municipal planning authorities. Central government requires such plans of city administrations in many countries. The logistics dimension of port capacity expansion is not a purely sectoral issue but requires coordination across government.

The Ministry of Transport is aware that more detailed assessment of landside transport infrastructure demand and investment requirements deep into the hinterland of the prospective new ports is needed and has begun consultations with the Ministry of Public Works to ensure the necessary capacity is developed in time. It also recognizes the need for regulatory changes to existing cabotage law and customs procedures to enable inspections inland.

Developing container terminals through concessions

This section reviews a number of the issues that arise when concessioning new terminals. Concession contracts have become the dominant model for private participation in providing port services around the globe. Chile adopted the model in the 1990's and has successfully attracted significant private capital investment to expand and renew its ports. As already discussed, operations in the container terminals developed through these concessions are efficient and productivity compares well with leading ports elsewhere. The general landlord port concession model was refined in Chile to assign pier and quay infrastructure provision as well as cargo transfer operations to concessionaires. The Port Authorities can only step in to construct piers when the bidding process fails to award a concession. Some bidding rounds have stalled, but no authority has stepped in as bidding is seen as the critical market testing stage in planning port expansion. The Port Authorities and Ministry of Transport carry out forecasting and strategic planning to determine the general schedule of demand for new capacity but the ultimate decision of when to invest is left to the market. Concessionaires take the demand and revenue risk. Public funds for capital investment are not exposed to this risk. The existing bidding system has proven to work well in Chile and appears generally well suited to concessioning terminals in a new large port.

How many terminals?

Expansion of container port capacity can be delivered through one terminal or multiple terminals, and in the latter case these can be located in a single port or distributed across two or more ports, depending on local circumstances. For expansion projects of one M TEU per annum or more there is a potential to split facilities between two or more terminals, subject to the scale sufficient to generate interest of potential terminal operators in bidding for the concession. A site that exceeds one million TEU with a quay length of 950 meters is likely to attract global operators. This size is also big enough to attract a diverse array of ancillary services that create local added value around the port. Smaller scale terminals, e.g. around 500 000 TEU, tend to attract local rather than global operators. For efficiency, terminals should be structured so that two vessels can be handled simultaneously. Accommodating large vessels implies larger concessions.

The size of the projects under consideration in Chile allows for multiple large terminals. At San Antonio, the project would accommodate four 1.5 M TEU terminals. The Valparaiso project would accommodate two 1.5 M TEU terminals.

Who is eligible to bid?

Explicit port competition policy and general antitrust competition policy will determine if existing terminal operators are eligible to bid for a new concession and whether acquisition of the new concession would require divestment of some existing interests. Competition is important to avoid the development of monopoly rents and to drive efficiency, creating pressure on prices and service quality. Competition can take place between separate terminal operators within a single port or between ports serving overlapping hinterlands. Both forms of competition exist in the ports serving the Santiago region and competition is evident with examples of shipping lines switching operations between San Antonio and Valparaiso and between terminals in San Antonio.

There was a consensus among participants that the presence of three different terminal operators competing in a port or in overlapping hinterlands secures adequate competition. More competitors are desirable only if this doesn't compromise economies of scale. Two or more operators also provides for resilience should one suffer a natural disaster, strike or other interruption to operations. San Antonio and Valparaiso each have one consolidated terminal operator plus one new entrant, awarded a construction and operation concession within the last three years.

The new terminals might be larger than existing concessions, each of which amounts to an approximate capacity of 1.0 million TEU per annum. They may therefore offer economies of scale, and may attract an international terminal operator vertically integrated with a shipping line. Issues and opportunities for coordination with existing concessions therefore arise. Opening a new large terminal may reduce the value of existing concessions.

If the new terminals have a significant technical potential to be more efficient than the existing terminals, ensuring competition between terminals in the new port will be as important as overall levels of competition in the region if maximum benefits are to be passed on to users of the new terminals and to the economy as a whole. As noted, the size and configuration of the San Antonio project is particularly well adapted to promoting competition and economies of scale. Terminals should be opened successively. Terminals 1 and 2 should be let to different operators. When terminals 3 and 4 are concessioned (Figure 1.7), the operators of 1 and 2 could be eligible to bid with a view to extending integrated operations into terminals 3 and 4 respectively. The Antitrust Authority would have to approve such extensions. In many configurations the holders of today's concessions at both ports could be eligible to bid without undermining the three operator minimum for adequate competition in the region.

Figure 1.7. **Schematic representation of new large port at San Antonio**

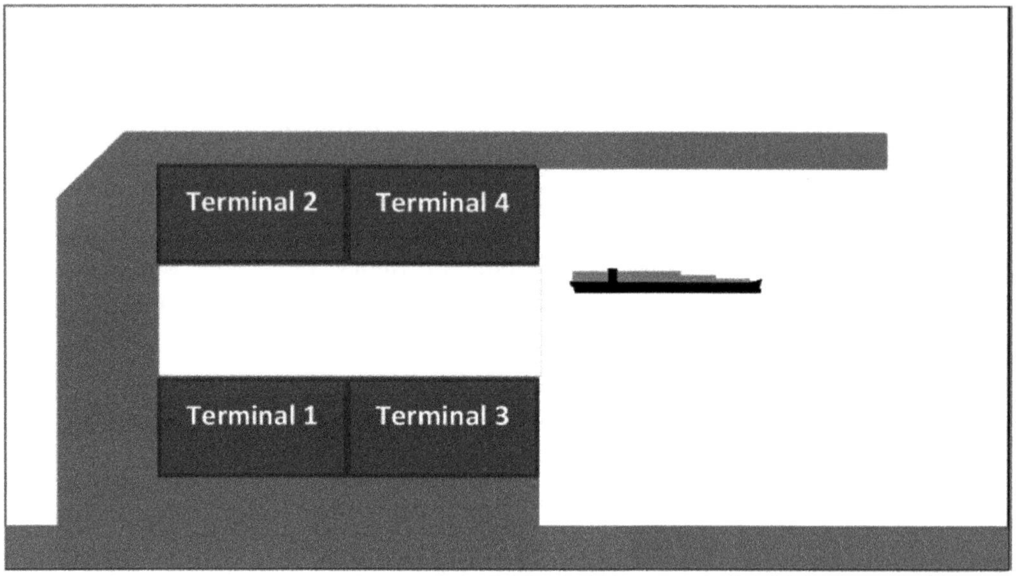

Issues of market exit are an integral part of concessioning. While privatisation increases efficiency in the short-term, one needs to secure conditions for the long-term as well. In the case that operators decide to leave the market before the end of the concession, governments that have not foreseen this possibility might find themselves spending significant public funds and renegotiating from a disadvantageous position.[9] Thus exit clauses need to be considered when structuring the project.

Quay and breakwater construction

Ports require large capital investments in infrastructure – quays, piers, breakwaters – that take many years to recoup. The lumpiness of these sunk investments has led to many jurisdictions to develop systems of concessions where government funds basic infrastructure. There is, however, no universal model and in the United Kingdom, for example, investment in some ports is purely private. Moreover, different parts of the infrastructure have different life-spans (measured in decades for quays, centuries for breakwaters).

In Chile, the terminal operator invests in piers and quays. As noted, port authorities are allowed to develop pier and quay infrastructure only when the bidding process fails to deliver a concession. No port authority has so far invested in piers in Chile as a failure of the bidding process is taken as a signal that there is no business case for the project. Landlord port models elsewhere in the world generally assign investment in quay and pier construction to the port authority. The Chilean approach may increase the cost of port infrastructure to the extent that the cost of private finance exceeds public finance and transaction costs tend to be higher with concessions and public private partnerships but this appears to be outweighed by incentives to complete construction on time and to budget. Prior to the introduction of concessioning the public sector had a poor record of delivery, with long delays and consequent cost overruns. Guasch (2013) reports that on average 75% of publicly financed infrastructure projects in Latin America experience cost overruns with the mean overrun about 35%. The bidding process for port concessions in Chile has so far escaped problems of grossly over-optimistic revenue forecasts associated with many concessions and public private partnerships for transport infrastructure elsewhere. The assignment of responsibility for financing piers to concessions also has the advantage of countering any tendency to over-invest taxpayer resources in port infrastructure in order to compete with rival neighbouring ports.

Constructing breakwaters is an integral part of many port capacity expansion projects. This fundamental part of the port infrastructure has a life span that extends well beyond that of a container terminal concession. Concessioning breakwater construction jointly with a terminal concession would be complicated with more than one terminal operator. It creates risks that are difficult to price when terminals are built sequentially: one terminal operator would set the charges for the breakwater to be paid by the other. Therefore, breakwater projects are commonly unbundled from terminal construction and the bidders for financing the breakwater are excluded from bidding on the terminals.

Unbundling allows port authorities to finance breakwaters and charge terminal concessions for its use on an equal basis. Construction might be financed directly or via a separate concession. Technically, because of the simple structure of the project, either option can be used. The interest in opting for direct investment is to minimize the cost of finance. The interest in private finance for the breakwater would be to transfer construction risk to a company with a recent track record in construction of similar projects (the last major breakwater built in the central region of Chile dates from the early 1900s). A concession would also take the burden of paying for construction in the short term with repayment over a very extended period off the books of the Port Authority (although the liability still resides ultimately with government).

The cost for building a breakwater for one of the major ports under consideration is small compared to the substantial gain of economic prosperity foregone if the project were not to be built. There was consensus among roundtable participants that unbundling breakwater construction from terminal concessions would facilitate timely development of a new port and is compatible with the objectives of competition policy.

Concluding comments

Key points for strategic planning of port development

Summarising much of what precedes, public policy makers and port authorities need to undertake the following strategic analysis in support of cost-benefit assessment and decision making on container port investment.

1. Conduct a disaggregate analysis of prospective demand as a basis for forecasts that cover a realistic range of scenarios. This includes:
   - Evaluating existing terminal offerings, with benchmarking on the basis of recognised performance measures, to determine if there is congestion and if productivity improvements and/or investment in cargo handling technologies and information technology are likely to increase capacity over the longer-term.
   - Estimating project demand using scenarios to evaluate potential trends beyond 10 or 20 years, calibrating forecasts with historical data but also identifying potential shifts in population, economic growth, location of activity and new business opportunities in sectors where the country has solid competitive prospects and including potential constraints on the further developing of existing trade. Identifying potential breaks in consumption patterns beyond the incremental effects of growth in population and per capita incomes is included here.
2. Understand the container shipping market. This includes:
   - Identifying the captive part of the container market.
   - Analysing which cargoes the container terminals will serve so that hinterlands are understood and opportunities for local value creation are to be identified.

- Assessing the ability of expanding the shipping market, through changes to regulations (e.g. cabotage, removal of non-tariff barriers) and through modal shift from truck or rail to short sea shipping.

3. Consult with shippers, carriers, logistics businesses, current port concessions and other cargo interests to understand their perspectives on the best way of expanding container port capacity. Identify critical issues that must be addressed for success. This includes:

   - Developing an integrated approach of infrastructure planning for both hard infrastructure and logistics services.
   - Including social and environmental issues in planning (impact on the quality of life, emissions, congestion, etc.).

4. Clarify of what kind of port and/or port terminal is envisaged. This includes:

   - Making decisions on port type: Gateway, hub, or feeder? Common user or dedicated terminal? Are the goal economies of scope or economies of scale?
   - Finalizing which of the broad possibilities remain, e.g., expansion of capacity by (a) modernising existing facilities, (b) adding to existing facilities or (c) developing a greenfield project?

5. Reserve land to be used for land side port operations, rail and road access, warehousing, logistics and distribution services and hinterland transport infrastructure.

Roundtable discussions underscored the importance of forecasting demand for port services that examines the potential drivers of growth and goes beyond extrapolation of trends or focusing on aggregate GDP as a basis for long-term forecasts. Past performance is often a poor indicator of the future; global shipping markets, export markets, domestic consumption and import markets are all undergoing change. This creates uncertainty that forecasting can only address through the development of scenarios to test plausible changes in the markets most relevant to the region served by the port.

For central Chile the Roundtable discussion highlighted three considerations of particular relevance to making forecasts of demand for container port services more robust:

1. As average household incomes rise in middle income countries and a middle class with more discretionary disposable income expands, there can be rapid change in the structure of demand with a shift from export-dominated traffic to a greater share of imported consumer goods.
2. Refrigerated exports of fruit and vegetables are a staple of current container traffic with great potential to grow. The preference of shippers of these goods for direct services is a significant factor in the decisions of shipping lines on network configuration. There are potentially external limits to the growth of this sector, availability of irrigation water for example, that are worth examining to make forecasts more robust.
3. Maritime container traffic can also be generated by modal shift from truck to sea and internal growth of short sea shipping. Both would be stimulated by a relaxation of restrictions on cabotage. As well as increasing port traffic, resulting feedering opportunities would make operation of large container vessels in Chilean ports more economic.

It is never too early to bring in stakeholders, particularly cargo owners (not just exporters but also retailers and agricultural producers), to get a market-based sense of the reality of the forecasts. Understanding the requirements of cargo interests grows more important as value creation for the participants in the supply chain becomes the primary factor in network redesign. This means cargo interest requirements need to be studied (to identify market-specific requirements), and both shipping lines and cargo interests need to be involved in the port expansion and hinterland infrastructure planning. Demand forecasts tend to be buffeted by unanticipated game-changers and those who pay for transport are often aware of them ahead of government.

There is an important role for developing Key Performance Indicators (KPIs) in relation to congestion designed to monitor the development of capacity constraints and also identify opportunities to improve the productivity of existing facilities. Port productivity benchmarks can be used to identify whether the existing berth and yard productivity meet international standards, or could be increased with smaller scale investments than construction of new berths. In the Chilean case, it was clear that both San Antonio and Valparaiso have reached a high level of productivity, confirming that capital investment in additional terminals is the only way to expand container services. New terminals will be constructed to accommodate the largest ships expected to enter service on the West Coast of South America, which exceed current maximum berth depths.

Figure 1.8. **Relevant factors in liner network configurations**

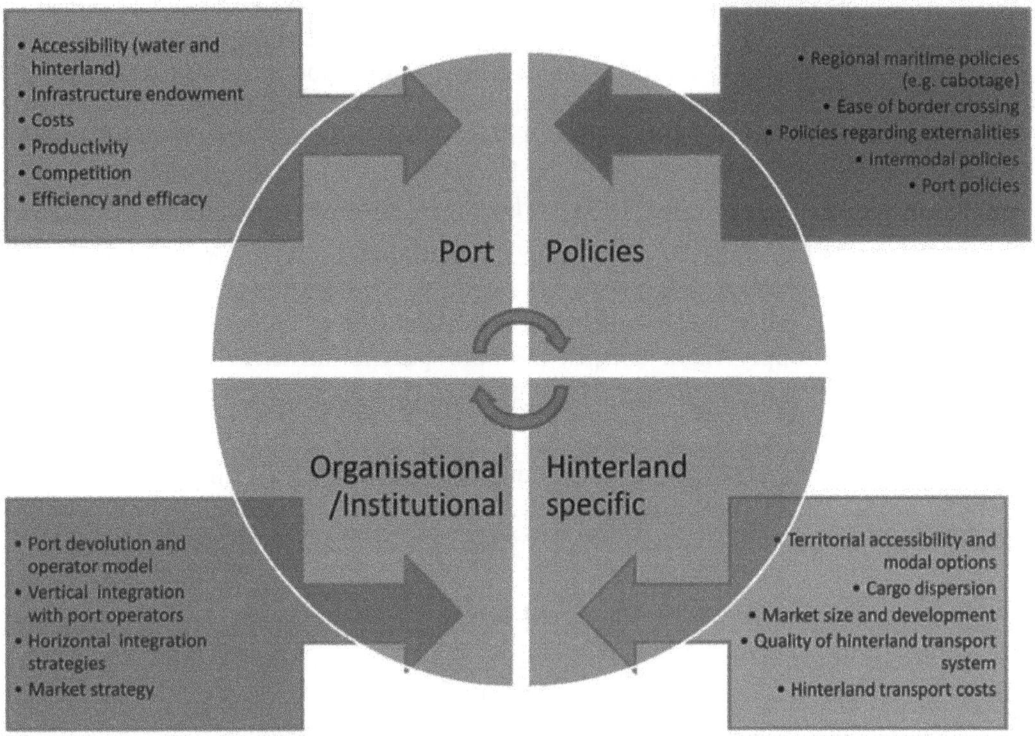

Source: Wilmsmeier (2013), roundtable presentation.

The key factors that determine which ports shipping lines call at are summarized in Figure 1.8. Beginning in the upper right corner of the figure, the roundtable focused on the importance of aligning regulatory policies, both landside and maritime, to remove impediments to growing trade, such as inefficient border controls, restrictive cabotage policies and weakly defined strategies for development of the logistics industry, a factor that is particularly important where ports compete for business as hinterland access has become the focus for global supply chain competition.

All four quadrants of the figure require monitoring and the development of a small set of key performance indicators to monitor quality of service from both port and government perspectives are recommended. For example, baseline highway statistics might be used to monitor the quality and capacity of the hinterland transport systems. These can identify the extent to which bottlenecks in existing highway infrastructure will be exacerbated by putting additional port traffic on the roads. The indicators developed can also be used to measure improvement by port investment but also hinterland investment and policy initiatives.

Measuring the performance of a logistics system is a considerable challenge and very much a product of what data a country already collects, and what data it chooses to collect in future. Thinking about ideal

KPIs from a government perspective is best done through community consultations with relevant supply chain partners. Many port businesses already measure KPIs to track continuous improvement, but consider sharing their KPIs in public as divulging competitive strategies. That said, there are already efforts underway by ports and individual partners to develop KPIs that are useful in measuring some parts of the performance of a logistics system, and some KPIs that are already collected globally. In addition to the Journal of Commerce Port Productivity KPIs previously discussed that demonstrate port productivity (upper left quadrant in figure 8) at San Antonio and Valparaiso, many ports evaluate their infrastructure endowments as adequate for existing vessel sizes, collect data on changes in port traffic as a ratio to economic growth, and so on. For the upper right quadrant, many governments rely on the indicators provided by the World Bank Doing Business (Trading Across Borders) database[10] or the Logistics Performance Index database[11] and select comparable countries to benchmark against. These indicators are problematic as small countries and large ones are not necessarily good equivalents and a country like Chile, given its geographical features, may not find reasonable comparators. There are very few appropriate benchmarks for the lower left quadrant, as this is mostly about developing appropriate policies and institutions, while those in the lower right are quite country-specific. The development of appropriate KPIs is an area Chile may consider exploring via stakeholder consultation in the process of developing its logistics and freight policies. There are many examples to draw on, and this could be an area for future research on options suitable for Chile's specific hinterland configuration.

Roundtable participants agreed that hinterland investment may be as important to the competitiveness of a terminal as on-port investments, given the inter-relationships between port capacity, congestion and reliability. This reinforces the earlier discussion about alignment of regulation and hinterland infrastructure so as to optimise the whole supply chain not just the port-specific infrastructure. Failure to consider the whole supply chain risks port investments by simply moving reliability issues and bottlenecks outside the gate rather than addressing them as part of the whole project.

The four quadrants in Figure 1.8 are interconnected and the weak links need to be identified, establishing which factors are a brake on business development: logistics policy, competition policy, restriction of cabotage, trade restrictions, customs, sanitary inspections, IT systems, and so on.

Expanding container port terminal capacity in Chile

To meet growing demand in a dynamic economy, the Chilean Ministry of Transport and Telecommunications is planning for large-scale container port capacity expansion. The Ministry's analysis of demand and options for the location and design of the port are thorough and in line with the steps set out in this report for robust assessment of the economic case for investment. Some additions to the consultations and analysis undertaken would reinforce the quality of the preparations. These could include a more detailed look at the requirements of cargo interests in the region, particularly with respect to their assessments of the realistic growth potential of their businesses over the life span of the project. Discussions with the Antitrust Commission would be useful for developing a common view on the minimum number of concessions and operators for adequate competition in the market at a relatively early stage, to allow time for reflection in parallel with the other work preliminary to launching concessions.

Developing a national/regional freight and logistics plan that integrates port expansion with hinterland infrastructure development. Hinterland infrastructure will require investment in step with port expansion if it is not to become a bottleneck in supply chains and if road congestion is to be contained. There might be potential for establishing a dry port and logistics centre in the vicinity of Santiago, connected to the new port by rail.

Completion of the national freight transport and logistics strategy will be important in providing the confidence required for private investment in infrastructure, in the hinterland as well as in the ports. Consultations with local communities affected by port development on managing environmental and other external costs should begin at the earliest stage possible. The approach adopted by the Port Authorities of planning expansion in phases that minimise demand/revenue risk and facilitates competition by providing for two or more terminal operators in each port is eminently appropriate. Chile's port concession model has proved successful and is suited to the larger scale investments planned. The port concession law also appears to allow for breakwater infrastructure to be financed separately from terminals and quays, which would simplify concessions for terminals in a major new port.

Notes

1. Modernisation of State Ports Act (Law 19.542).
2. In the top 20 ports in the Americas for berth productivity, San Antonio is currently rated as having a berth productivity index of 43, above that of Manzanillo in Mexico (42) but below that of Lazaro Cardenas, Mexico at 65 (page 9, Journal of Commerce (2013). The best practice port in the Americas is Long Beach at 74, showing that there is always room to improve productivity by benchmarking business processes against best in class.
3. In 2013 bunkering costs are on average six times more the bunkering costs of 2000; ibid.
4. Source: www.alphaliner.com
5. Source: www.alphaliner.com
6. Examples of new terminals within this range are found in Asia (i.e. Jebel Ali new Container Terminal 3, due to open next year, has an annual capacity of 4 MTEU; Port of Ennore, India 1.5 MTEUs), Europe (COSCO terminal in Piraeus increases to 3.7 MTEU in 2015) and America (Puerto Cortes, Honduras, 1.8 MTEUs).
7. The road: rail trade-off in terms of cost efficiency is between 500 and 750 kms according to Resor et al. (2004); in Canada, the distance is considered to be one-half day's driving distance by truck.
8. Freightliner http://www.portoffelixstowe.co.uk/partner-directory/rail-companies/freightliner/
9. The case of Busan in Korea is illustrative. The two then congested terminals were concessioned to two global terminal operators (Hutchinson and PSA respectively). This was the first foreign investment allowed in the sector. After 5 years, however, these operators left for various reasons. It took another five years for local market operators to develop competitive services. Meanwhile the national administration had to assume responsibility and the expense of keeping the terminals open.
10. http://www.doingbusiness.org
11. http://lpi.worldbank.org

References

Acciaro M. and McKinnon A. (2013). Efficient Hinterland Transport Infrastructure and Services for Large Container Ports. OECD/ITF Discussion Paper 2013-19.

Ashar and Rodrigue, 2012, The Geography of Transport Systems, Hofstra University, Department of Geography. http://people.hofstra.edu/geotrans/eng/ch3en/conc3en/containerships.html.

Australian Customs and Border Protection Service (2012). Annual report 2010-11.

Caprile R.M. (2013). Developing a Successful Port by Concessions. Irish Ports Association 2013 Conference, September 2013, Dublin Ireland.

Davies, Philip (2009). Container Terminal Reservation Systems, Paper presented at the 3rd Annual METRANS National Urban Freight Conference, Long Beach CA, 2009.

De Langen P.W. (2008), Ensuring Hinterland Access: The Role of Port Authorities, JTRC OECD/ITF Discussion Paper 2008-11.

EU (2010), Transport Research in Chile, European Union Programme of the International Relations Department at CONICYT, Santiago 2010.

European Commission (2013). Proposal for a regulation of the European Parliament and of the Council establishing a framework on market access to port services and financial transparency of ports, COM(2013) 296 final, Brussels, 23.5.2013.

Freightliner (2013) 'Written Evidence to Parliamentary Inquiry' http://www.publications.parliament.uk/pa/cm201314/cmselect/cmtran/writev/ports/ports.pdf

GHK and Royal Haskoning (2008). Felixstowe Port Logistics Study for Suffolk Coastal District Council, 2008.

Giuliano G., and O'Brien T., (2008). Responding to Increasing Port-related Freight Volumes: Lessons from Los Angeles/Long Beach and Other US Ports and Hinterlands, JTRC OECD/ITF Discussion Paper 2008-12.

Guasch, J. L., (2011). Logistics as a Driver for Competitiveness in Latin America and the Caribbean, presented at the fifth Americas Competitiveness Forum for the IADB and Compete Caribbean, Santo Domingo, Dominican Republic, October 5-7.

HPA (2012) Hamburg is Staying on Course: Port Development Plan to 2025, Hamburg Port Authority 2012.

International Transport Forum (2008). Port Competition and Hinterland Transport, OECD Publishing 2008.

International Transport Forum (2009). Integration and Competition between Transport and Logistics Businesses, OECD Publishing 2009.

International Transport Forum (2013). Better Regulation of Public Private Partnerships for Transport Infrastructure, OECD Publishing 2013.

Jara-Dıaz, S, Tovar, B and Trujillo, L (2008), On the proper modelling of multioutput port cargo handling costs, Applied Economics, 2008.

Journal of Commence (2013). Key findings on terminal productivity performance across ports, counries and regions. July 2013.

Kaselimi, E.N., Notteboom, T.E., Pallis A.A., and Farrell, S. (2012). Minimum Efficient Scale (MES) vs. 'Preferred' Scale of Container Terminals. Research in Transportation Economics, 32(1), 71-80.

Koppenjan, J.F.M., & Leijten, M.. (2007). How to Sell a Railway: Lessons on the privatization of Three Dutch Railway Projects.European Journal of Transport and Infrastructure Research (Online), 7(3), 201–222.

Michea A. (2013). Puerto de Gran Escala – The case for a new container terminal in central Chile. OECD/ITF Discussion Paper 2013-20.

Monios J. (2011). The role of inland terminal development in the hinterland access strategies of Spanish ports. Research in Transportation Economics 33, 59-66.

OECD 2010, Transcontinental Infrastructure Needs to 2030 / 2050, North -West Europe Gateway Area - Port of Rotterdam Case Study, OECD Futures Programme 2010.

Resor, R.R., J.R. Blaze and E.K. Morlok (2004). Short-Haul Rail Intermodal: Can It Compete with Trucks? Transportation Research Record, 1873, 45-52.

Resor, R.R. and Laird, P.G. (2013). Railroad privatization and deregulation: Lessons from three decades of experience worldwide, Research in Transportation Business & Management, 6, 1-2.

Rodrigue J-P, Debrie, J. Fremont, A. and Gouvernal E. (2010). Functions and Actors of Inland Ports: European and North American Dynamics. Journal of Transport Geography, 18 (4), 519–529.

Slandebroek W. (2013). Container liner shipping: Trends and development, Mare Forum, Amsterdam, 22 October 2013.

Thompson, L., and Kohon J. (2012), Developments in rail organization in the Americas, 1990 to present and future directions, Journal of Rail Transport Planning and Management.

Tovar, B and Wall, A (2012) Economies of scale and scope in service firms with demand uncertainty: An application to a Spanish port, Maritime Economics & Logistics (2012) 14, 362–385.

UK DfT (2011). Department for Transport, Transport Statistics Great Britain 2011.

U.S. Department of Transportation - Maritime Administration (2013). Panama Canal Expansion Study: Phase I Report: Developments in Trade and National and Global Economies. November. US: Washington D.C.

Vidaud M. & de Tilière G., 2010, Railway access charge systems in Europe, 10th Swiss Conference on Transport Research - STRC 10, Monte Verità / Ascona, septembre 2010.

Wilmsmeier, G., Monios J and Perez G, (2013). Port System Evolution – The Case of Latin America and the Caribbean, Proceedings of IAME Annual Conference 2013.

Wilmsmeier, G. (2013). Liner Shipping Markets, Networks and Strategies. The implications for port development on the West Coast of South America. The case of Chile. OECD/ITF Discussion Paper 2013-22. And presentation: http://www.internationaltransportforum.org/jtrc/RoundTables/2013-Container-Shipping/WilmsmeierShippingMarketsSlidesOct2013.pdf

Chapter 2

Puerto de Gran Escala (PGE)

Alexis Michea[1]

The Government of Chile is developing a national ports development plan. The plan is outlined in this paper and its implications for strategic development of hinterland transport infrastructure capacity are discussed. The paper reviews port capacity and sets out the legal framework for competition between port terminal concessions and the assignment of responsibilities between port authorities and terminal concession holders for investment in new facilities. Forecast demand is compared with projected container terminal capacity and plans for development of a new large container port development, a Puerto de Gran Escala (PGE), are outlined.

1. Ministry of Transport and Telecommunications, Santiago, Chile

Chilean ports overview

Currently, there are 56 ports in Chile. They can be grouped in three categories:

- 10 state-owned, public use ports, distributed along the entire coastline, from Arica near the border with Perú to Puerto Natales and Punta Arenas in the vicinity of Cape Horn.
- 14 privately owned public use ports, with terminals developed by private companies. These ports transfer containers as well as bulk cargos, and are located in the bays of Mejillones (north of the country), Quintero (centre) and Concepción (centre-south).
- 32 privately owned, private use ports. These are terminals developed by private companies whose core business is not port operation (for example, coal power plant operators) or developed by companies under contract to large freight generators (for example, copper mines). Located in a variety of zones along the coast.

Figure 2.1 illustrates the geographic distribution of state-owned ports and the volume and composition of freight handled.

The state-owned sector was modernised in the late 1990s by means of Law 19 542, which divided the large national ports company (Empresa Portuaria de Chile, Emporchi) to create 10 independent port companies (Empresas Portuarias), each with its own board of directors, management, etc. These independent companies have a mandate to ensure efficient port operation and development whilst maintaining a sound financial status. The Law establishes a regulatory framework for freight transfer operations to be carried out by private companies, which can operate under two different regimes:

'Mono-operador': a single concessionaire operates an entire terminal, and

'Multi-operador': multiple agencies operate within a terminal administered by the respective port company.

The Law also establishes a general rule under which new pier infrastructure can only be developed by private companies and through public tendering. Only in the event of an unsuccessful tender can the port company itself invest.

Some of the smaller ports operate without a terminal concession, entirely under the multi-operador regime. Currently, 7 out of the 10 public companies have concessioned terminals under the 'mono-operador' regime, with at least two further companies planning tenders for terminals within the next year or so. Several of the companies in the group of 7 are developing plans to concession second terminals within a similar timeframe.

16 years after the reform of the public ports sector, the Chilean model is considered a largely successful experience, both because of the financial results that public and private companies involved have achieved, and because of the quality of the port facilities, services and rates on offer.

Figure 2.1. **Freight transferred in Chilean state-owned ports (tonne/year)**

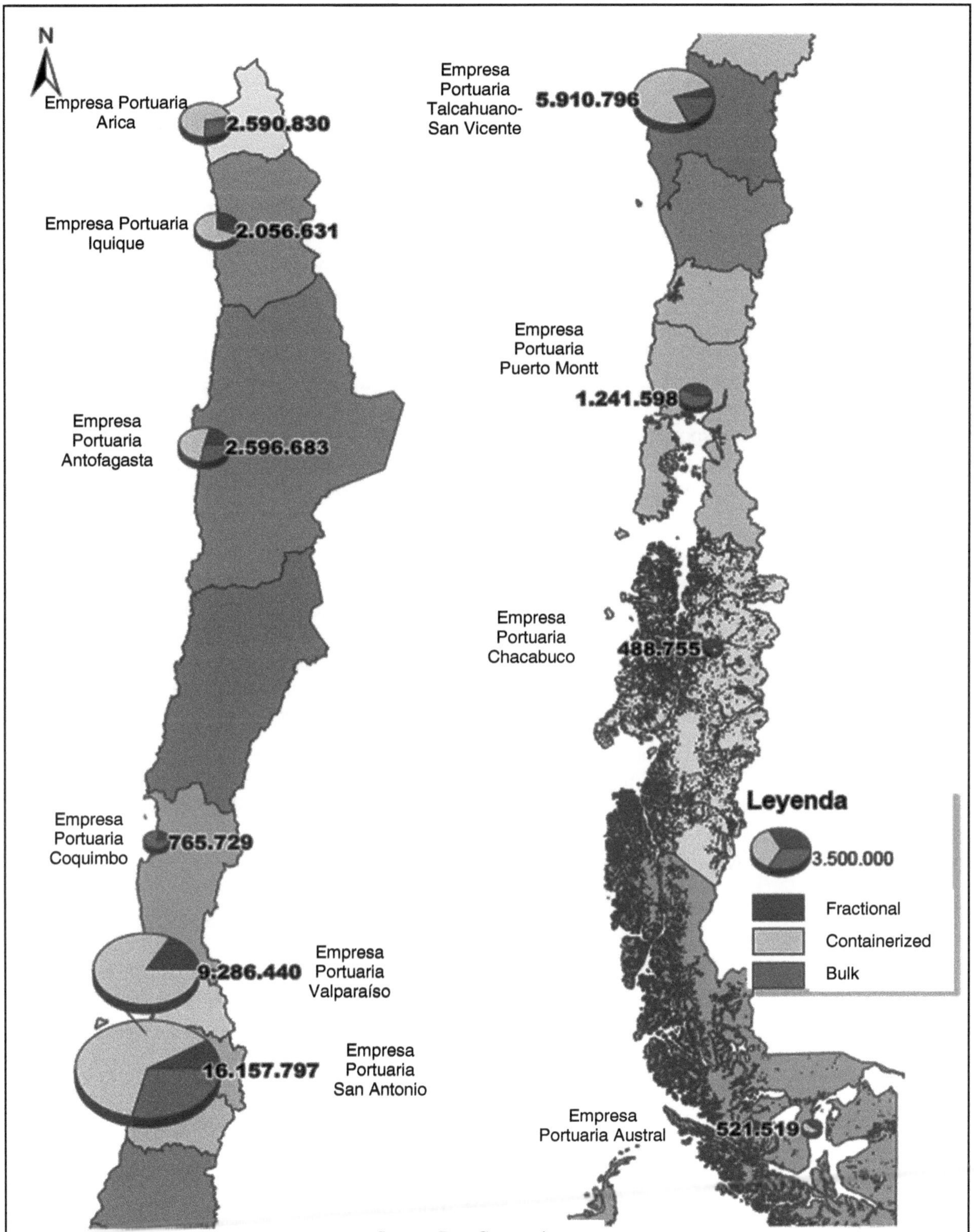

Source: Port Companies.

Planning and development in the state ports sector

The Law also mandates that each company maintain an updated 'Master Plan' and 'Referential Investment Schedule' for its continuous and timely development. These instruments typically address issues such as expected demand levels in the respective hinterlands, pier infrastructure and equipment needs. With few exceptions, issues relating to the port's connectivity and the impact of freight movement on the road/railway network are not considered.

A case can be made for this to change. From an operational point of view, a terminal's effective capacity is not only determined by the transport stages that occur within the port boundaries, but also by those upstream: from port gate to linkroads, through the urban road network in the host city, to long-haul trunk roads and railway lines connecting the port with its clients. Efficient and sustainable development of these parts of the freight transport system depends on integration with port development plans and will benefit from engagement of the port companies in broader hinterland development strategies. Contributing to integrated strategic planning will help guarantee the long-term competitiveness of the terminals under their responsibility.

At a higher organisational level, the Law did not create a national ports authority but gave the Ministry of Transport and Telecommunications (MTT) a central role in overseeing, and in some cases powers to approve or reject, specific stages of the independent planning, development and management processes of port companies. Examples of the areas for such intervention are modifications to the physical area where each company has legal responsibility for developing port facilities (known as 'Recinto Portuario'); emitting non-binding opinions on tendering conditions; and setting the board of directors legally-binding yearly management goals (the 'Planes de Gestión Anual', PGAs).

Additionally, the Law sets the responsibility for MTT to propose 'strategic plans' for port development. Although the law does not specify exactly what such plans should cover, the ministry has taken a view that they should address all the aspects that independent port authorities do not have the mandate or incentive to take on themselves, for example with regard to coordination of plans for the long term development of ports which share large portions of hinterland.

Towards a national ports plan

The case for integrated planning, the historical criticism levied at the ministry for its abandonment of its infrastructure planning role in the freight sector in general, as well as other responsibilities that the Law establishes for MTT (e.g. safeguarding mutually beneficial port-city relationships), has guided the ministry in its current drive for developing a national-scale port planning instrument, the National Ports Development Plan (PNDP, by its initials in Spanish).

Work on the PNDP started in 2012, with the following objectives:

1. To complement the independent companies' mid and long term planning:
   - Harmonising company plans, and
   - Including aspects which might so far have been omitted.
2. To ensure the preparation of investment plans for the port system in its entirety, i.e. including:
   - Road and railway solutions, as applicable, within port cities,
   - Road and railway solutions, as applicable, to connect with each port's hinterland, and
   - Logistics support infrastructure, intermodal exchanges, etc.
3. To ensure that state-owned ports play their role as key link in the development of each of the country's regions to the full, catering for the needs of all relevant economic sectors.
4. To ensure the progressive building of local consensus and thus continuity in development plans, clearly identifying stakeholders and responsibilities in pushing forward such development.

The elaboration of the PNDP has been organised into three main stages:

Stage I: Review and critical analysis of current port planning instruments, i.e. port company Master Plans, with regard to four main aspects:

a) Demand forecasts for each freight type expected in the Region in the foreseeable future;

b) Port infrastructure necessary to meet such demand;

c) Coastal space needed for future development; and

d) Identification of road and rail needs.

Stage II: Update and standardisation of long term demand forecasts, modelling of freight distribution between ports with overlapping hinterlands, identification of requirements for coastal space reserves and sheltering works necessary for long term development, and identification of the freight transfer needs that the state-owned port system might not be able to fulfil.

Stage III: Public discussion of the Stage II proposals with regional and national stakeholders and generation of the first formal version of the PNDP.

Stage I was completed in May 2013, with Stages II and III scheduled for the months of October and December, respectively. The design of the PNDP foresees regular updates, the first of which is due in December 2014; these updates should progressively broaden the scope of the development issues covered, moving on from an infrastructure-oriented effort to one which also comprises aspects such as the potential need for improvements to the institutional framework.

Work on the PNDP is being carried out in conjunction with individual port companies under the coordination of the ministry. MTT will also undertake specific components of the analysis and liaise with other state organisations; this, for example, is the case of trunk road analysis in the central region currently being carried out with the Ministry of Public Works.

Puerto de Gran Escala (PGE)

Within the general planning framework set out by the forthcoming PNDP, there is a project that, given the economic importance of the hinterland it will serve and the magnitude of the infrastructure involved, stands out as singular. Its working title is Puerto de Gran Escala or PGE (which can be translated as 'Large Scale Port').

The hinterland of interest is central Chile. It comprises five of the country's Regions[1], including Santiago, the national capital and the major cities of Rancagua, Valparaíso, Viña del Mar, La Serena and Coquimbo. The area is responsible for 60% of national GDP and is home to 66% of the country's population. Among other types of freight, it produces a significant volume of agricultural products for export and generates significant demand for imported retail goods. Most of the freight is transferred in containers, with average traffic in the last three years (2010-2012) totalling 1.9 million TEU/yr.

There are currently two container ports in the Valparaíso Region: San Antonio and Valparaíso. Their location is illustrated in Figure 2.2 overleaf, together with a general view of each.

Both are mainly import/export facilities, with figures of 94% and 98% foreign trade for Valparaiso and San Antonio[2] respectively. The remainder is a mixture of cabotage and freight in transit to/from Argentina. Each port currently has two terminals for freight transfer. Table 2.1 shows the total volume of containers transferred during 2012 by terminal.

Table 2.1. **Containers transferred in the Valparaiso Region (TEU/year)**

Terminal	2012
Valparaíso Terminal 1	930 174
Valparaíso Terminal 2	12 473
San Antonio Terminal 1	1 067 846
San Antonio Terminal 2	1 425
TEUs transferred in total	2 011 918

Source: Regional statistics provided by EPV for year 2012.

According to the Latin American and Caribbean ranking of container transference (CEPAL 2012), Valparaíso port ranks 15th with San Antonio port in 13th position. If they are considered as a single 'greater port' (both ports being close substitutes catering for largely overlapping hinterlands), they rank 5th, between the ports of Cartagena (Colombia) and Manzanillo (Mexico).

Figure 2.2. **Existing container seaports in central Chile**

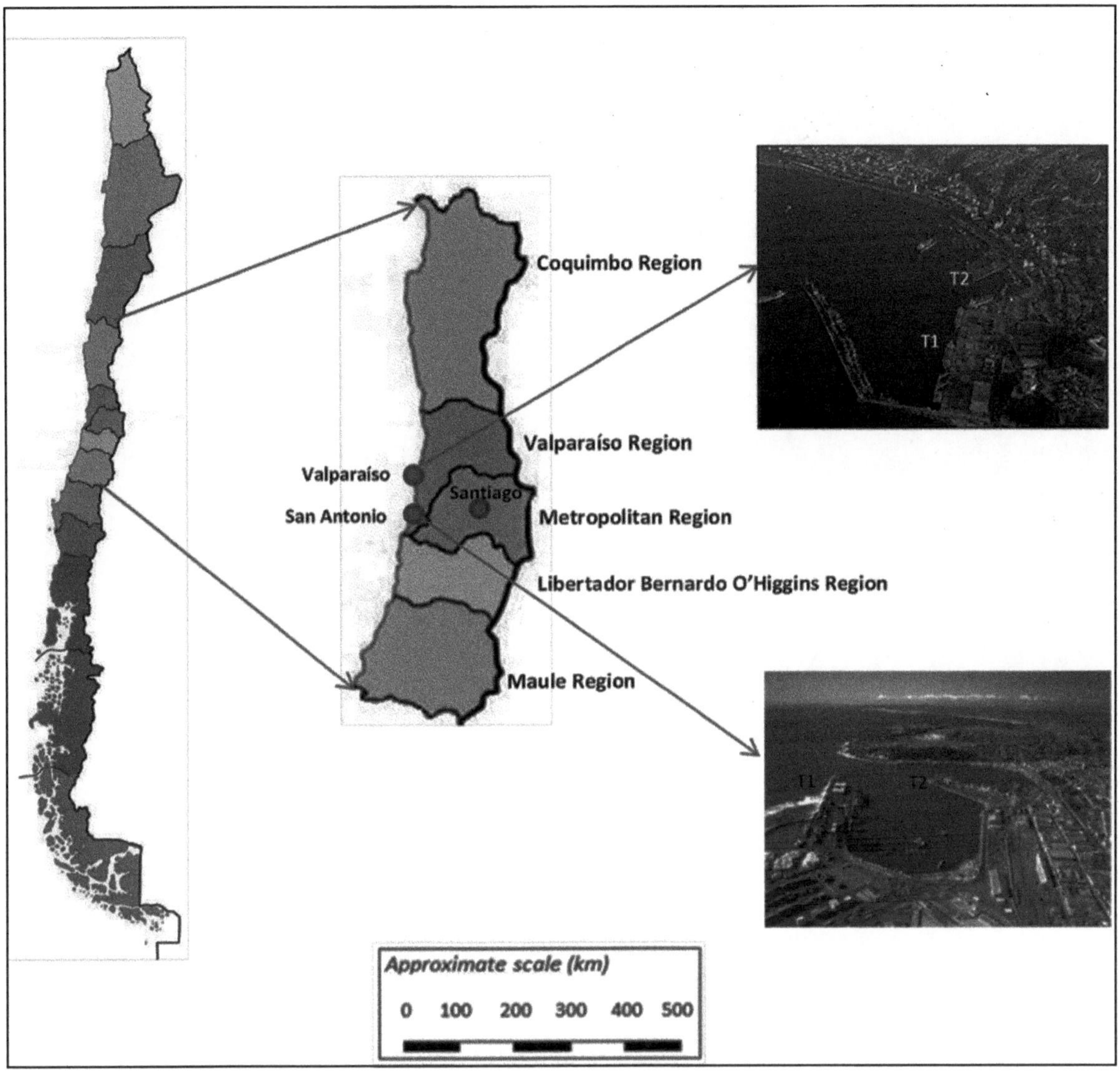

Source: Port Companies.

Figure 2.3 illustrates the layout of main roads and railway lines connecting Santiago with the ports in the Valparaiso region.

Figure 2.3. **Trunk roads and railway lines connecting ports located in the Valparaiso region with Santiago**

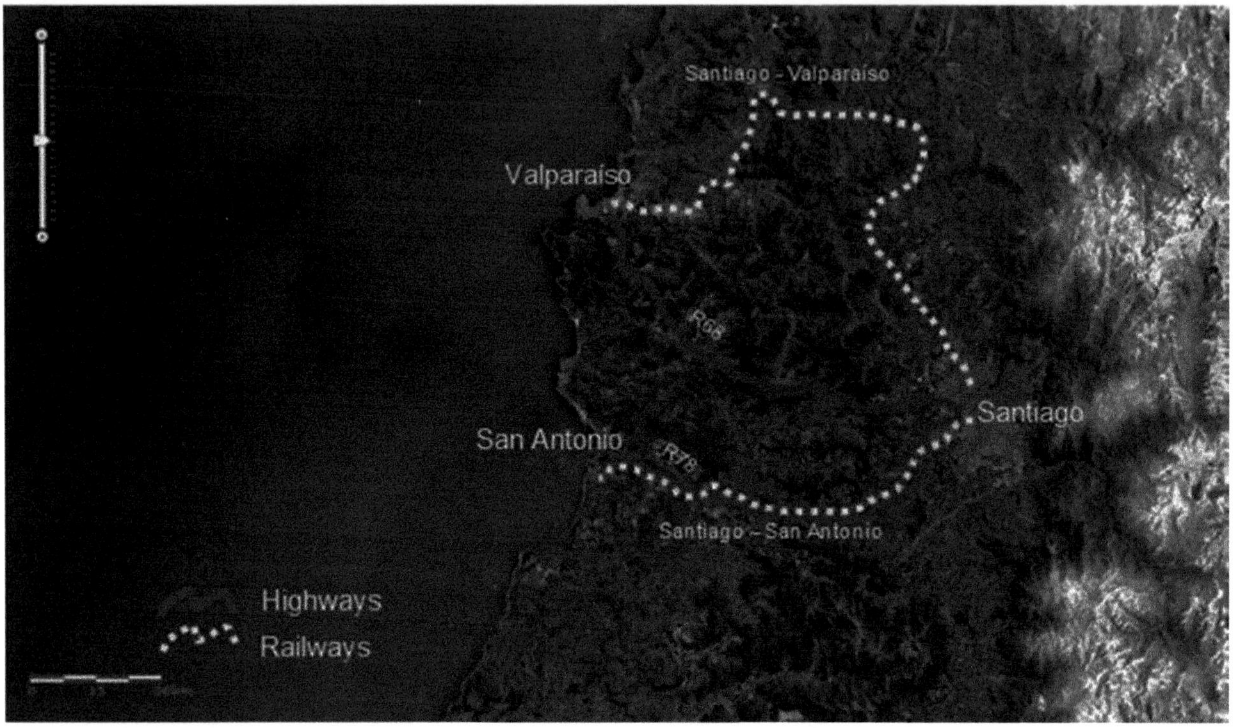

Source: Ministry of Transport and Telecommunications, Chile.

The main roads connecting the inland with the coastal port cities in the Valparaíso Region are two concessioned motorways, i.e. Routes 68 and 78, both themselves connecting at Santiago with Route 5, the backbone of national north-south connectivity by road. Route 68 connects Santiago with Valparaíso port with 119 km of very good standard two carriage motorway, including two tunnels (Lo Prado and Zapata). Route 78 connects Santiago with San Antonio port over a distance of 110 km, another very good standard two carriage motorway and no tunnels. Two-way Annual Average Daily Traffic[3] (AADT) measured in 2012 on Route 68 (at the Zapata toll, located 59 km from Santiago) was 29 845 pcu/day and on Route 78 (at the Melipilla toll, located 66 km from Santiago) was 15 212 pcu/day.

There are also two railway lines connecting Santiago with the ports in the Valparaiso region. The railway connecting Valparaiso port with Santiago has a length of 187 km, operated by locomotives with a haulage capacity of 1 200 tons, with 15 car trains running 5 convoys per week. This accounts for less than 2% of Valparaiso port's total freight transfer.

In contrast, the railway line that connects San Antonio with Santiago, with a length of 110 km, moved over 710 000 tons in 2012, accounting for 22% of unpackaged freight and 3% of the containers transferred by San Antonio port.

The container transfer capacity currently available in the Region is estimated at 2.3 M TEU/yr., more or less evenly distributed between:

- Terminal 1 in the Port of Valparaíso, operated by concessionaire TPS; and
- Terminal 1 in the Port of San Antonio, operated by concessionaire STI.

The main characteristics of TPS and STI quays are displayed in Table 2:2:

Table 2.2. **TPS and STI quays main characteristics**

	TPS quays Valparaiso					STI quays San Antonio		
QUAY	1	2	3	4	5	1	2	3
Quay length (m)	188.5	200	231.5	230.5	152.2	263	253	253
Total linear length (m)	620			382.7		769		
Draft (m)	13.8	13.8	13.8	9.4	9.4 -8.5	13.50	11.34	11.34
LOA (m)	142	200	229.5	230.5	107.5	363	253	253
Year of investment / improvement	1998-1999	1998-1999	1998-1999	-	-	1995	1995	1995
Dock equipment	5 Gantry cranes + 2 Gottwald cranes			-	-	6 Gantry cranes		
YARD								
Total area (ha)	9.55			5.51		30.4		
Covered area	10 800	-	-	-	-	0.5		

Source: Regional statistics provided by EPV and EPSA for year 2013.

The respective state port companies, Empresa Portuaria San Antonio (EPSA) and Empresa Portuaria Valparaíso (EPV), have successfully tendered their second container terminals in recent times:

In 2011, EPSA awarded the 'Costanera-Espigón' project to the Puerto Central concession; and

In 2013, EPV awarded the 'Terminal 2' project to OHL Concessions.

The Puerto Central and Terminal 2 projects, as they are commonly known, will add a total of 1 500 m of pier length through a total investment of US$ 830 M, increasing the nominal installed capacity in slightly over 2 M TEU/yr. This, plus small increases provided by minor infrastructure improvements to the existing terminals operated by TPS and STI (i.e. approximately 100 m pier extensions), should bring the total capacity in the region to approximately 4.9 M TEU/yr. by 2021.

Demand forecasting

As part of the preparatory work on PGE, in 2011 MTT commissioned a study with the aim among other things of reviewing and updating econometric modelling of demand. The study was finished in May 2012.

Using historical data up to 2010, the analysis sought to explore various model specifications, assess its statistical goodness-of-fit, and recommend a model on which to base further analysis regarding infrastructure needs, cost-benefit appraisal, etc.

The study tested the following explanatory variables, which were selected based on both the availability of historical data and the estimated feasibility of subsequently producing exogenous forecasts with which to forecast freight transfer:

- National and regional GDP (Valparaíso Region)
- GDP by economic sector and Region within hinterland

- GDP of foreign countries and/or economic zones to where Chilean exports are shipped
- Population
- GDP per capita
- Copper exported through the Valparaíso Region.
- Month and quarter dummies to represent seasonality

In terms of model structure, two main variants were tested:

- Linear Model

$$DemTon_{mont\ h,year} = a_0 + \sum_i a_i \times VE_{i,year} + \sum_{mont\ h} a_{mont\ h} \times d_{mont\ h}$$

- Multiplicative Model

$$\ln(DemTon_{mont\ h,year}) = a_0 + \sum_i a_i \times \ln(VE_{i,year}) + \sum_{mont\ h} a_{mont\ h} \times d_{mont\ h}$$

Where:

$DemTon_{mont\ h,year}$, represents the demand in tons for a specific month of a year

a_i, are the parameters determined by the regression for each variable

$VE_{i,year}$, is the value adopted by the predictor variable i, each year

$d_{mont\ h}$, dummy for the month or quarter

These two structures were used to generate both aggregate container traffic estimates and sector-specific ones (agricultural, copper and iron, wine and others).

Given the information available, several regressions were made considering the different valid combinations between the model structure (linear/multiplicative, month/quarter) and sets of predictor variables. Table 2.3 summarized the results for the three models that delivered a coefficient of determination over 90%.

Table 2.3. **Analysed models**[4]

	Intercept Value	GDP Elasticity	GDP_per_Capita Elasticity	Copper Elasticity Region	R2
Model 1	-21.52 (-19.5)	1.98 (32.1)			91.23%
Model 2	10.56 (99.1)		2.68 (31.8)		91.06%
Model 3	-25.64 (-12.9)	1.90 (27.6)		0.4 (2.5)	91.66%

Source: Development of a Port Demand-Capacity Model for the Valparaíso Region", GreenLab for MTT, May 2012.

The demand forecasts arising from these three models are illustrated in Figure 2.4.

Figure 2.4. **Estimates from models 1, 2 and 3 (base: GDP growth 3%)**

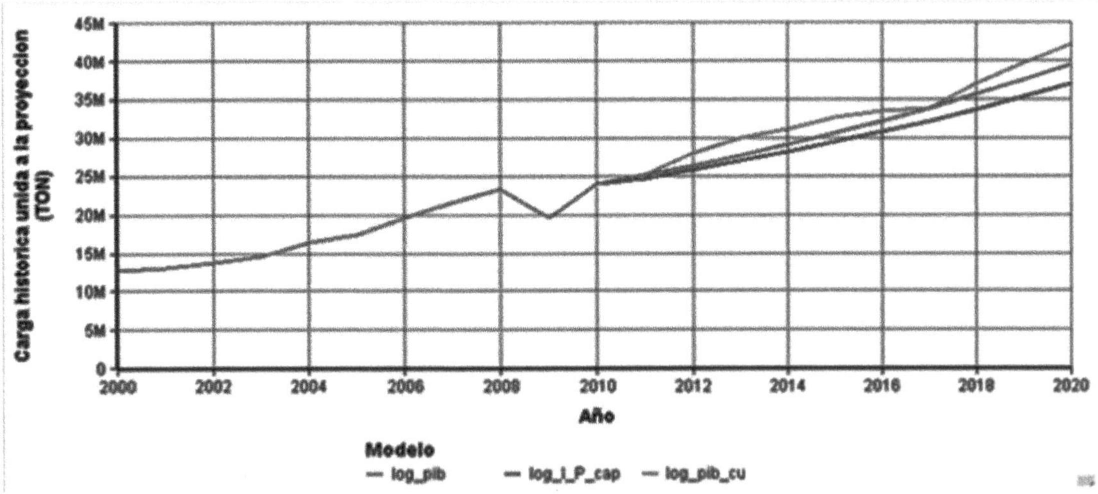

Source: Ministry of Transport and Telecommunications, Chile.

Figure 2.4 shows that Model 2 (GDP per capita as predictor variable) produces the lowest estimates, followed by Model 1 (pure GDP) and finally Model 3 (pure GDP & copper production). The non-smooth nature of the latter is explained by step changes in the explanatory variable derived from specific mining projects.

Analysing the demand forecasts for different scenarios, Model 2 turned out to be the one with the least dispersion in the results as shown in Table 2.4. Therefore Model 2 was selected for the following analysis.

Table 2.4. **Results for year 2020**

Scenario	Model 1	Model 2	Model 3
Low growth	33.3 Mton	33.0 MTon	35.7 Mton
Moderate growth	46.9 Mton	41.3 Mton	49.7 Mton
High growth	39.5 Mton	36.9 Mton	42.1 Mton

Source: Development of a Port Demand-Capacity Model for the Valparaíso Region, GreenLab for MTT, May 2012.

For the purpose of the policy implications under consideration, it is important to note that, even with these demand estimates, which could be considered to lie on low part of the spectrum, the argument in favour of swift action towards public tendering of new infrastructure seems strong. This is discussed in more detail in the following section.

Balance between demand and capacity

Figure 2.5 illustrates the balance between nominal capacity and projected demand as per Model 2.

Figure 2.5. **Demand and capacity: Existing and projected container terminals in the Valparaíso region**

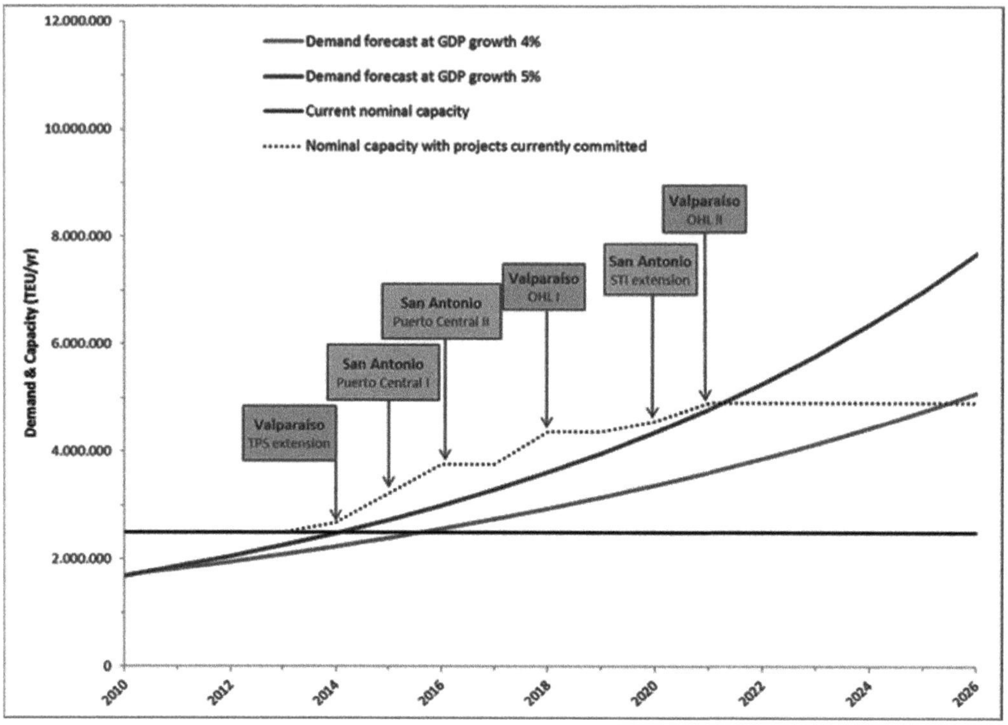

Source: Ministry of Transport and Telecommunications, Chile.

According to these demand forecasts, at an average GDP growth[5] of 4%, the total nominal capacity in the port system would be exhausted around 2025, whilst at a rate of 5% this would happen in 2021[6]. The elasticity considered for both, blue and red line, was 1.98.

As part of subsequent analysis carried out by MTT in conjunction with EPSA and EPV, the demand estimates shown in Figure no. 5 were again revised; this time, the goal was to do some initial exploration as to the real capacity of the hinterland to generate the freight volumes predicted by the 'black box' of the econometric model. In summary[7], the results are slightly more conservative than those contained in Figure no.5, with a demand forecast lying between the red and blue lines, much closer to the blue one, with GDP growth of 4.5% and elasticity of 1.65. Under this scenario doubling of demand would occur a year later, i.e. while 10 years were needed to double demand in the previous analysis, 11 years are needed in the later analysis.

In any case, the main conclusion of this analysis is that, at some point in the first half of the 2020s, simply as a result of underlying demand growth, it is likely that Central Chile will need additional container transfer capacity.

The need to advance rapidly

In the view of MTT, there are at least four main reasons which make advancement on the new PGE project a priority:

- The scale and complexity of issues posed by engineering challenges, environment permit approvals, port-city relationships, etc., imply long time spans between preparation of tenders and inauguration of the first terminals in the new port. This will be the first time since the early 1900s that new breakwaters will be built in the country, so there is no recent experience on a project of this nature, and certainly not within a systematic environmental approval process such as the one in force, introduced two decades ago.
- The fact that existing terminals could face some degree of obsolescence as a result of changes to the merchant fleet serving the region, i.e. the advent of large post-panamax vessels, which may require not only longer dock lengths but also deeper ports as shown in Figure No. 6 (Valparaíso currently has an authorised draft of 11.4 m whilst San Antonio has a draft of 12.4 m – see figure 2.6 for the evolution of container ship drafts).
- The potentially catastrophic consequences that severe port congestion could have on foreign commerce for a country that generates 38% of its GDP from exports (OECD average being 27%; all data from 2011). The exact effects of congestion in the Valparaíso region are uncertain but, for example, could include ships being diverted 500 km south to ports in the Concepción Region (thus imposing on freight the additional cost of longer journeys by heavy goods vehicle) and/or the introduction of 'congestion fees' such as that imposed in Chennai (India) in 2011, where charges between USD 75 and USD 145 per TEU were reported[8].
- The unknown economic and strategic consequences of a potentially significant fraction of Chilean exports being forced to rely on feeder services to Callao (Perú).

In turn, the costs of advancing swiftly are considered comparatively low; approximately US$ 2 M have so far been spent on studies, for a project than could cost as much as US$ 2 750 M, i.e. less than 0.1%. MTT is hence taking what can be considered a prudent stance: in the face of potentially serious consequences for the economy and relatively low costs for 'buying insurance', let us all just move as quickly as possible.

Figure 2.6. **Evolution of new generation container ships**

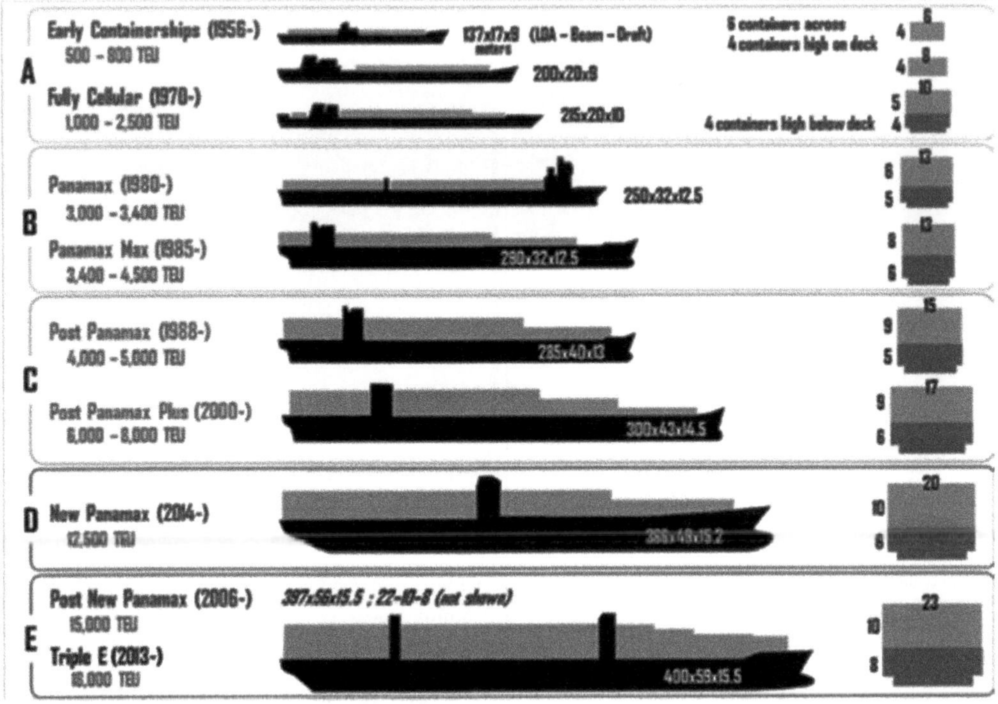

Source: Ashar and Rodrigue, 2012. All dimensions are in metres. LOA: Length overall.

Work so far

The ministry has actively pursued parallel progress by both port authorities on preparatory studies for public tendering of a single alternative; the choice between alternatives to be made at a later stage, based on the technical evidence produced by such studies. Work began in early 2011 with an analysis, carried out by MTT, to identify potential locations for a PGE-type project within a radius of approximately 150 km to the north and south of the existing ports. This produced three alternative locations.

Based on this work, in January 2012, EPV and EPSA were formally commissioned by the Minister to produce by the month of December the first stage of the technical studies necessary for an objective comparison of alternatives. At EPV's request, a fourth alternative was added to the initial three identified by MTT.

In December 2012, studies were presented to the MTT and SEP[9] authorities, including basic engineering, design, cost estimations, road and rail requirements in the port vicinity, preliminary project appraisal and legal analysis. As a result of these analyses of the four potential locations identified, two front-runners appeared: one in San Antonio, located a few hundred meters to the south of the existing terminals, and one in Valparaíso, located approximately 2 km to the north of Terminal 2, in an area commonly known as Yolanda.

PGE profile

To provide an idea of the size and configuration of the project, Figure 2.7 illustrates two of the alternative designs currently being considered.

Figure 2.7. **PGE alternative designs and key figures** (values are indicative, designs preliminary)

San Antonio	Valparaíso
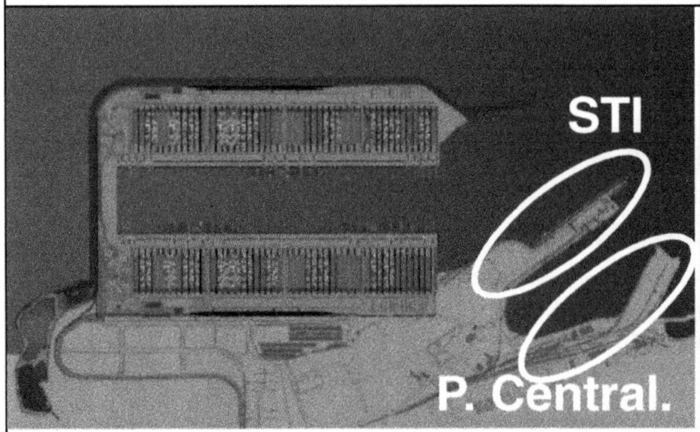	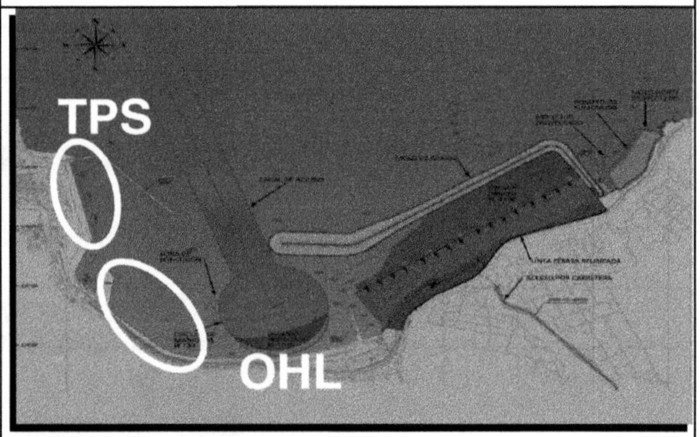
Design vessel: post-panamax of 400 m LOA Maximum total dock length: 3 560 m in two fronts Breakwater length: 3 700 m Backup area: 170 ha Nominal capacity: 6 MMTEU/yr. Estimated total investment: US$ 2 750 M	Design vessel: post-panamax of 400 m LOA Maximum total dock length: 1 770 m in one front Breakwater length: 2 300 m Backup area: 44 ha Nominal capacity: 3 M TEU/yr. Estimated total investment: US$1 420 M

Source: Ports of San Antonio and Valparaiso.

In summary, in its maximum size option and final development stage, the project would be equivalent to more than triple the capacity currently installed in the region and triple the investment committed by the two new concessionaires.

Work in 2013 and beyond

During 2013 work is progressing along two complementary lines: one technical (in an engineering/ transport planning sense) and one financial.

The first aims to produce definitive versions of basic engineering and project appraisal (both private and social), whilst the second is looking at the definition of a tendering model suitable for the type of port development that is PGE. This relates to the fact that the project considers providing artificial sheltering infrastructure, principally large breakwaters, which poses a number of questions. Could a 30 year concession provide efficient funding and financing for the breakwater, itself a large and potentially risky expenditure? Would it be it better to jointly tender the breakwater and port terminal, or to do it separately? Would the current bid-winning system, i.e. by lowest composite transfer rate offered (in US$), work well in this case?

In answering such questions, it will be crucial not to introduce distortions into a market which should, at that stage, have four independent operators. This is especially relevant in a scenario in which the government was committed to funding part or all of the breakwater cost.

The goal for 2013 is to finalise these analyses, so that government authorities can make a decision on the definitive location and instruct the selected port authority accordingly. If this is accomplished, an important step will have been taken towards publicly tendering the first terminal of the PGE by 2015. Delay beyond that would pose a serious risk to having the terminal operative in time.

Notes

1 The regions of Coquimbo (no. IV), Valparaíso (V), O'Higgins (VI), Maule (VII) and Metropolitana de Santiago.

2. Basis: tonnage

3. AADT is an indicator used in traffic analysis which measures the level of activity, in vehicles per day, of a given stretch of road. 'pcu' represents 'passenger car unit', an equivalence measure used to characterise a traffic stream composed of various vehicle types, using a common denominator.

4. Values in brackets are the t-statistic.

5. Reference Chilean GDP growth rates were 5.6% in 2012 and 4.5% on average in 2003-2012.

6. Ports in the Valparaíso region are already exhibiting some symptoms of congestion. For example, in 2011, a ratio of waiting time/service time of 16.8% was reported as average for the STI and TPS terminals, 10% being a broad 'best practice' reference figure. This translates into the conclusions drawn from Figure no. 5 being to some extent optimistic: the point where the capacity and demand curves intersect would possibly entail significant degrees of congestion.

7. For brevity a full account of the analysis has been omitted from this document but more details are available on request.

8. For illustration purposes, consider the case of a hypothetical 5 500 TEU ship on the route between Long Beach and Valparaíso, loading/unloading 1 200 TEU in the latter and currently facing total port costs of approximately 74 000 USD. A surcharge of 75 USD/TEU would result in an additional cost of 90 000 USD, thus more than doubling the total port cost of calling at Valparaíso. In the case of a hypothetical post-panamax vessel of 10 000 TEU capacity, assuming a transfer lot of 2 500 TEU, the 75 USD surcharge would result in an additional 187 500 USD per call.

9. The 'Sistema de Empresas Públicas', SEP, is an independent agency that monitors performance of state-owned companies, advises the Treasury on management decisions and sets financial goals for these companies. It is interesting to note that all 10 chilean port authorities have a sustained record of positive financial results.

Chapter 3

Liner shipping markets, networks and strategies:

The implications for port development on the west coast of South America

Gordon Wilmsmeier[1]

This paper analyses the evolution of liner shipping networks on the West Coast of South America (WCSA) and evaluates their impact on future port system development. The work describes the interrelationship between changes in scale and structure of trade and liner shipping network structures. Particular emphasis is given on ship size development, the emergence of refrigerated container trade and the evolution of market structure in the WCSA. Chile and the WCSA region more generally, face the challenges of market concentration, further evolution of liner shipping networks towards hierarchical networks driven by hub-and-spoke operations and the cascading effects of vessel redeployment. The paper underscores the necessity for institutional and private sector actors to act together and proceed based on integrated visions and strategies in order to achieve successful port development.

1. Economic Commission for Latin America and the Caribbean (ECLAC)

Setting the scene

This paper, predominantly on the challenges for port development, in some important sense cannot help but also be about the deeper phenomena of structural change in the maritime industry and geographical shift. The main objective is to analyse the evolution of symptoms of change in the liner shipping industry within South America and more particularly on the West Coast, as these changes are direct drivers of port infrastructure and port system development, which is both economically interesting and a matter of serious policy significance in its own right.

Port infrastructure and the quality of shipping services in a region or country are important determinants of countries' integration in the global market and their competitiveness. Given the sustained growth in emerging economies, despite the recent crisis, port infrastructure development has emerged as a crucial issue for future economic growth. The West Coast of South America (WCSA) and particularly Chile have experienced significant economic expansion over the last two decades. However, the role of infrastructure and its contribution to continued economic and social development has only recently returned to political agendas.

Growth in demand for port infrastructure, structural changes in the maritime industry and the changing geography of trade have clearly revealed the limits of the current transport infrastructure in the region and the country. Infrastructure development decisions, particularly as concerns port infrastructure expansion, are politicised, full of historicism and case-specific empiricism. Thus this work tries to stimulate a more systemic view to support more contextual, integrated and long-term policy decisions.

Wilmsmeier et al. (2013) identified critical moments in port development in Latin American and the Caribbean (LAC). Their work focused on the evolution of the port system in the region and its sub-regions. Their findings are the starting point for the present paper, which moves beyond the port to analyse the evolution of and changes in the maritime industry and, more particularly, liner shipping services on the WCSA. Beyond the critical moments identified in the previous work, this paper particularly focuses on the elements of technological change (related to ships), network strategies and liner shipping market structures.

Figure 3.1. **Critical moments in LAC port development, 1990-2013**

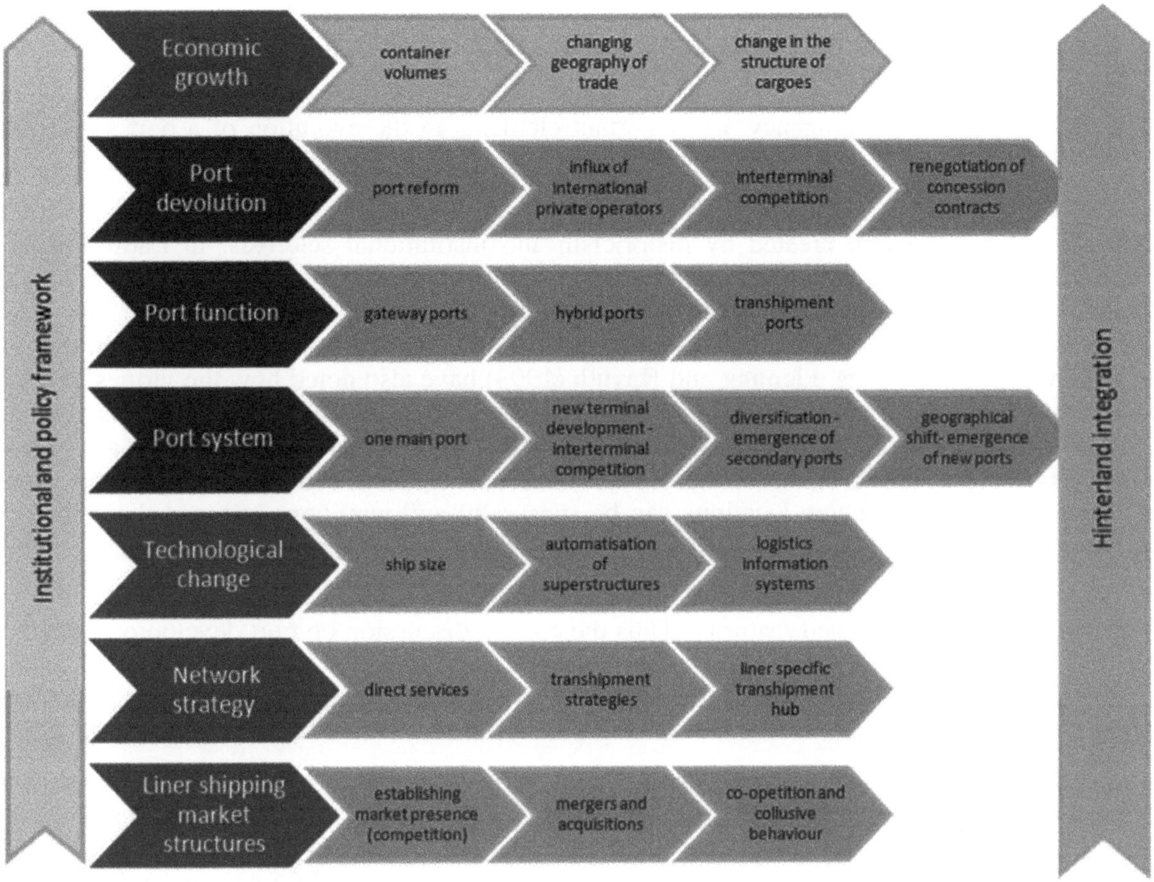

Source: Based on Wilmsmeier et al. (2013).

Port throughput development

Port throughput in Latin America and the Caribbean has grown from 10.4 million TEU (1997) to almost 43 million TEU (2012). At a compound annual growth rate of 9.9%, this development has put enormous pressure on port infrastructure in the region. However, in a global context LAC ports are only responsible for 7.2% of throughput, with all WCSA ports combined moving only about 1/6 of the TEU of the port of Shanghai.

The analysis of the WCSA port system by Wilmsmeier et al. (2013) hints that ports (represented by their actors, either public or private) were able to make use of critical moments more or less successfully. The port reform processes in the 1990s, notably in Chile, made it possible to advance port infrastructure development, particularly in terms of port productivity, and to initiate significant container terminal development through the involvement of the private sector. However, the sustained growth has brought the prevalent lack of port and transport and logistics infrastructure in the hinterland to light.

Thus far the focus has been almost exclusively on the development of main container ports, with only residual attention paid to secondary port development in the region. Similarly, port expansion planning is still usually port focused, not developed systemically. Hinterland transport infrastructure and logistical development are also not fully taken into account.

Path dependency and contingency are important elements in the evolution of a port system and its subsystems. Port devolution, competition and hinterland integration strategies, as well as public planning approval, are determinants in this context.

Path dependency is often created by historicism and institutional sclerosis. In Latin America the devolution process in many countries has left port development in the hands of the private sector. Wilmsmeier et al. (2013) refer to Swyngedouw (1992, p. 424e), who argues that "the production of locational effects as a result of capital investment in space", left to private investors, ignores important aspects when creating new ports. Fleming and Hayuth (1994) have also noted how the virtues of centrality and intermediacy that create strategic locations can be manufactured. The question is how this affects future private investment and institutional capacities of current development, particularly in a region where government investment in ports is almost absent. There seems to be clear evidence from the above analysis that the manufacturing of strategic locations can be successful and may have initiated the emergence of secondary ports in LAC.

Ports and port systems undergo lifecycles (Cullinane and Wilmsmeier, 2011) and on the WCSA the traditional main ports have reached maturity. Thus the current discussion on port development needs to be whether it is possible to extend the lifecycle of current locations and what solutions are available, or whether the development of a completely new site in terms of a locational shift is the best option to cater for future development and expansion of the existing port system.

Studies and political discussion on port development in the region have typically focused on the development of a single port, usually a country's main port, thus failing to recognise changes in the overall port system. Wilmsmeier et al. (2013) analyse the evolution of the LAC port system as a whole. Particularly, for the sub region WCSA and its East Coast counterpart (ECSA), the authors find clear indications of decentralisation processes. Over the last decade secondary ports have evolved much faster than the long-established main gateway ports in both sub regions. Thus there is a diversification of ports serving the demand for containerised trade, which is also accompanied by a geographical dispersion of ports.

In the case of Chile, the ports of San Antonio and Valparaiso handled more than two-thirds of the total containers moved within the country in 1997. By 2012, these two ports had more than tripled their throughput to over 1.8 million TEU. However, the overall share in container throughput of these two ports has fallen to just above 50%.

The ports of Talcahuano, San Vicente Terminal Internacional (SVTI) and Lirquén, all located in very close proximity, have evolved much faster than the traditional ports of San Antonio and Valparaíso. In 1997, SVTI did not even exist, and the others only played a minor role in the port system. In 2012, these three ports moved over one-third of all Chilean container trade.

Such diversification and geographical shift in the port system has occurred in parallel in Brazil and Mexico (Wilmsmeier et al. 2013). This diversification is being driven by the changes in the export structures and thus the emergence of new production centres in the South (especially for perishable products). Additionally, secondary ports are starting to engage in more integrated development strategies, which include consideration of logistics development connected to the port (e.g. Manaus, Brazil; Puerto Angamos, Chile).

Figure 3.2. **Evolution of container throughput in Chile, by port, 1997-2011**

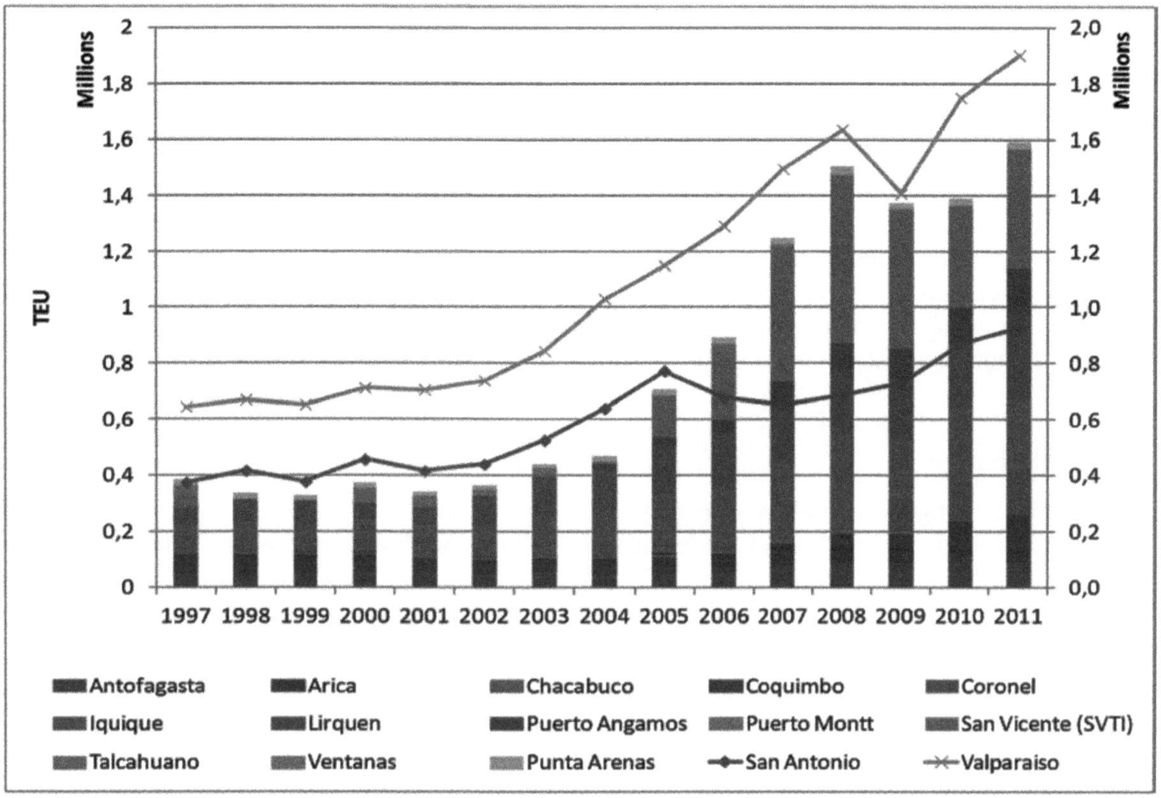

Source: Wilmsmeier et al. (2013).

The changes in the port system are relevant for Chile's future port development strategy for two reasons: a) expansion of production centres especially in the South but also in other parts of the country leads to a significant increase in hinterland traffic, not only to regional ports but also to the traditional main gateway ports, and b) the shift of economic activity can be expected to result in population increase in the affected regions, creating a new pattern of demand.

Strategies to deal with both factors include infrastructure development to cope with emerging and expanding markets and production centres. This can be achieved by expanding road infrastructure, significantly reinforcing the rail network or facilitating coastal shipping.

The available data suggest some evidence for a deconcentration of container traffic within the LAC port system, related to shifts both in gateway regions and from a gateway role to a transhipment role, thus supporting the movement of cargo through secondary LAC ports.

More research is required, but the shifts already identified have potential benefit for secondary ports, many of which are pursuing significant expansion to take advantage of the expected trends. These ports seek to reposition themselves within an emerging feeder market that could reduce the peripherality they experienced in the traditional LAC port and infrastructure system. The paper thus raises questions about port policy and both public and private sector responses to a changing LAC port geography.

Liner shipping

Analysis of port throughput and weekly capacity supply on the WCSA between 2000 and 2012 reveals a high correlation (0.9) over the whole period. However, the growth rates varied significantly and capacity supply grew faster than port throughput, particularly after the crisis. This section analyses the technological change, capacity development and market structure in liner shipping on the WCSA since 2000.

Technological change

Technological change in container shipping has unequivocally been a driver of port development. As shipping lines are seeking economies of scale, capacity adjustment has been reached mainly by deploying bigger vessels (Cullinane and Khanna, 1999). The following analyses technological change in terms of ship dimensions (capacity, draught, length and breadth) and its repercussions on port development in the WCSA.

The vessel sizes deployed on the WCSA and in South America in general have conventionally lagged behind the development in the principal trade routes (Perrotti and Sánchez, 2012). However, the evolution of vessel sizes and their TEU capacity dramatically accelerated from the second half of 2008. On the WCSA a significant difference exists between the routes crossing the Panama Canal (WCSA-Europe) and the other main routes (WCSA-Asia and WCSA-North America). In the case of the former, the Panama Canal is the limiting factor; since 2009 Panamax vessels have held an increasing share on this route. On the routes to Asia and North America (WCUS), where this limiting factor is absent, the biggest vessels now deployed can carry over 9 000 TEU; in 2008 the maximum vessel capacity was half that. At the same time the average vessel size (TEU capacity) is now above Panamax ship capacity. Figures 3 and 4 clearly depict the acceleration in growth of vessels' TEU capacity since 2008, and with that the cascading effect moving overcapacity from other main routes into secondary markets and thus replacing tonnage.

Figure 3.3. **Evolution of vessel capacity on West Coast South America main trade routes** (2000-12)

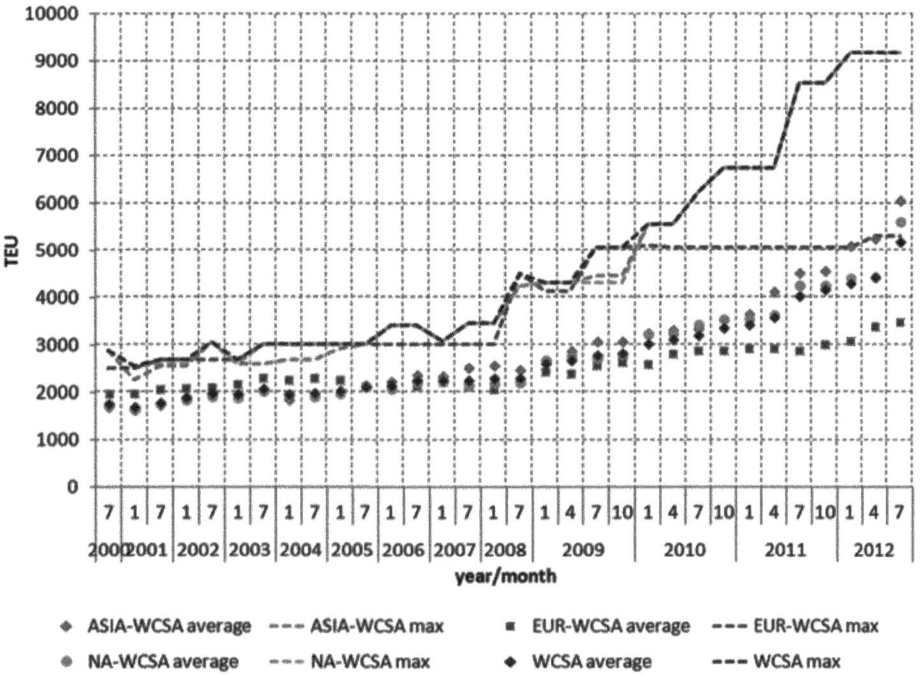

Note: The main trade routes are transpacific, transatlantic and Europe-Asia.

Source: Based on ComPairData, Lloyds List and Marine Traffic, various years.

Figure 3.4. **Evolution of vessel capacity on South American and other main trade routes** (2000-12)

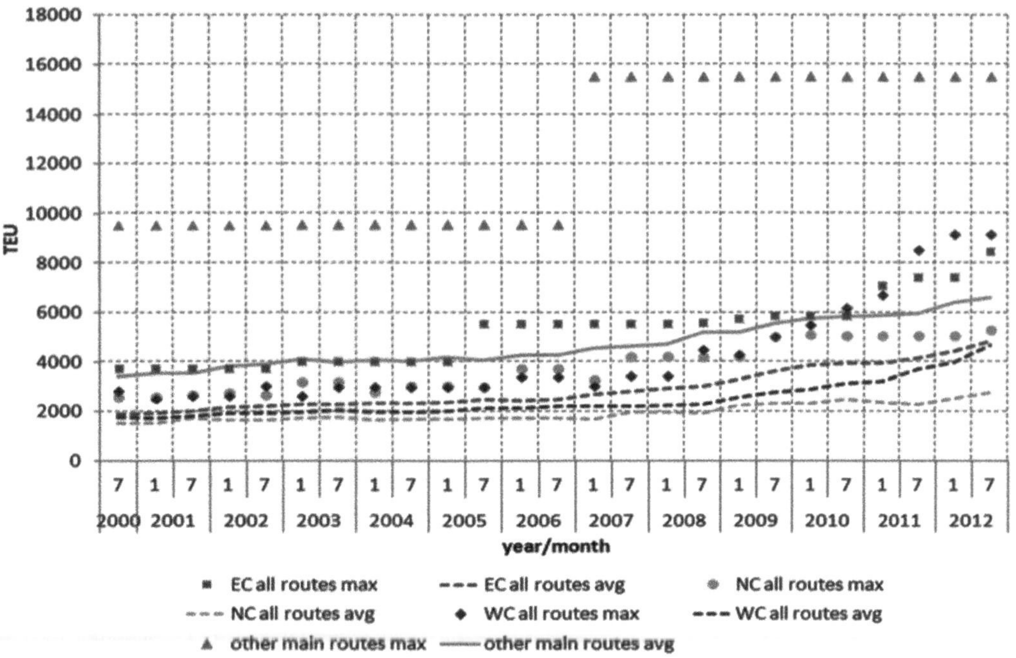

Note: EC = east coast; WC = west coast; NC = north coast; the main trade routes are transpacific, transatlantic and Europe-Asia.

Source: Based on ComPairData, Lloyds List and Marine Traffic, various years.

While there is much talk about the evolution of ship size and related future requirements for infrastructure, an analysis of the evolution of container ships since 2000 on the WCSA reveals that ships with a draught of 15m are already a reality. Further, even average draught of deployed vessels has increased by over 2m in the past 13 years. Thus, any new port development will have to consider vessel draught of at least 15m.

Figure 3.5. **Evolution of vessel draught on South American and other main trade routes** (2000-12)

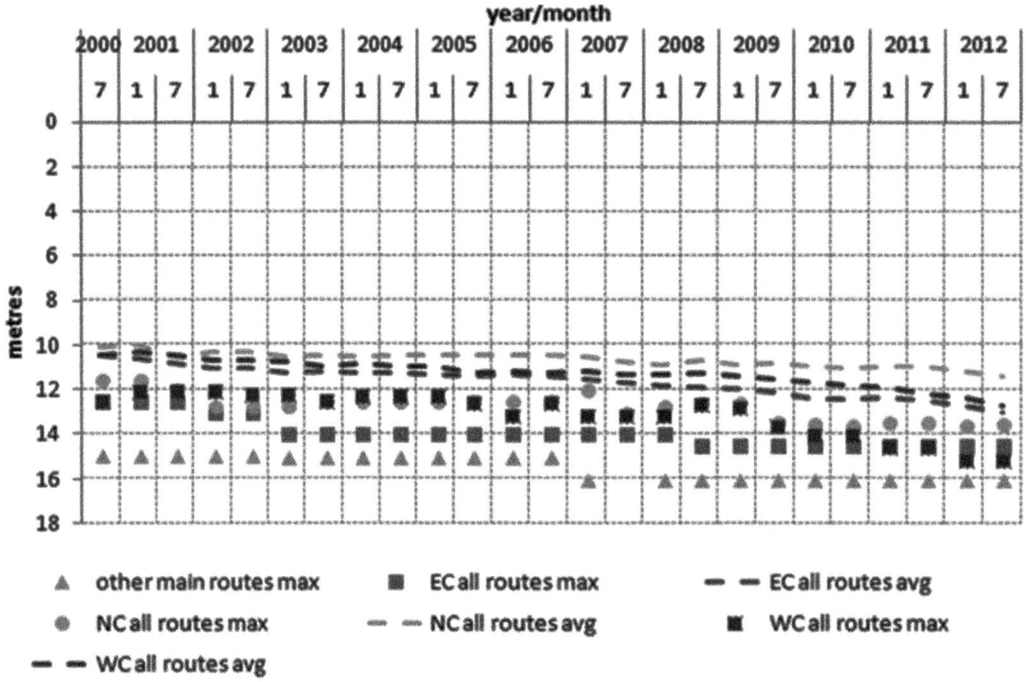

Note: The main trade routes are transpacific, transatlantic and Europe-Asia. The draught considered is the design draught of vessels fully laden.

Source: Based on ComPairData, Lloyds List and Marine Traffic, various years.

Vessel draught is only one aspect of the technological changes to ships that affect port infrastructure requirements. Additional aspects are ship length and breadth. The former determines the quay length and berth layout required to accommodate ships. The latter is a key indicator for superstructure requirements in ports, especially the reach of ship-to-shore cranes.

The average vessel length on the WCSA was above 250m in 2012, and the maximum vessel length reached 340m. In 2000 the maximum vessel length was just above 200m. Beyond actual length, variation in the length of ships serving a port is of high relevance to port productivity and to planning. Additionally, the breadth of vessels serving the sub region increased from 32.5m (2000) to over 45m (2012).

Figure 3.6. **Evolution of vessel length on South American and other main trade routes** (2000-12)

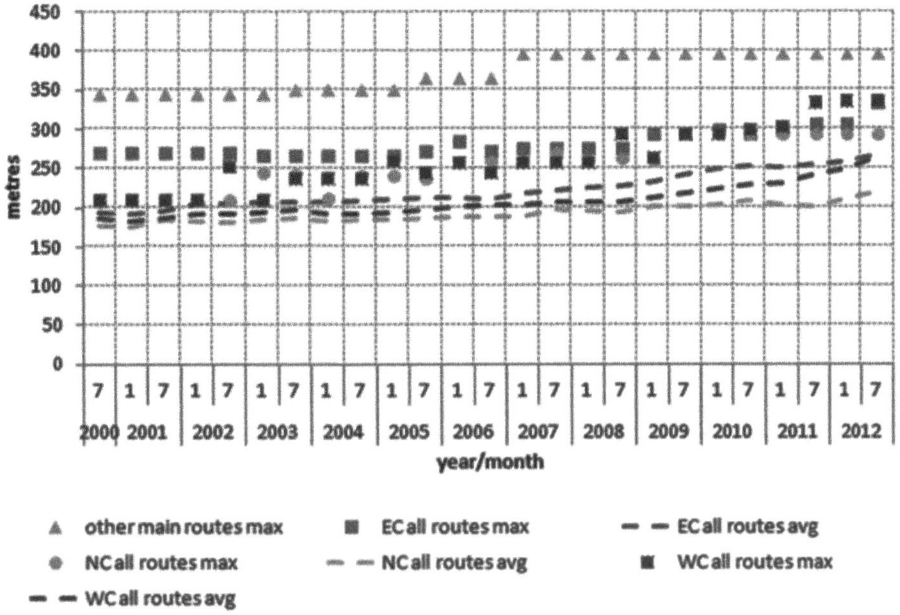

Note: The main trade routes are transpacific, transatlantic and Europe-Asia.
Source: Based on ComPairData, Lloyds List and Marine Traffic, various years.

Figure 3.7. **Vessel breadth on South American and other main trade routes** (2000-12)

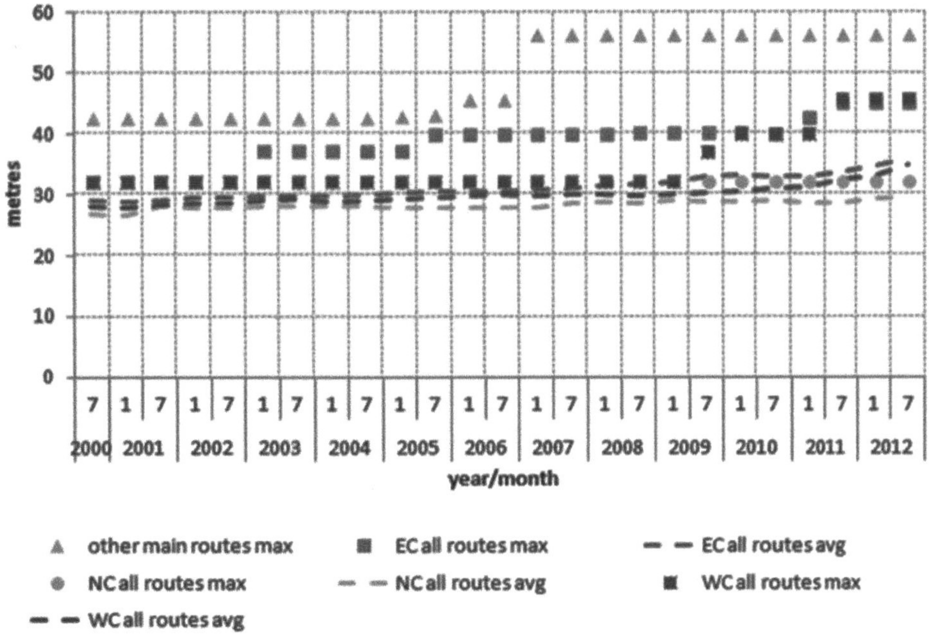

Note: The main trade routes are transpacific, transatlantic and Europe-Asia.
Source: Based on ComPairData, Lloyds List and Marine Traffic, various years.

The observed changes on the WCSA clearly show an acceleration of technological change, particularly since the beginning of the crisis in 2008. At the same time they illustrate the multidimensionality of technological change affecting port development and future port plans. The observations indicate increasing pressure to adjust port infrastructure to present requirements, as well as emerging pressure for new port development. A recent study expects 13 000-TEU ships to start calling regularly on the coasts of South America between 2016 and 2020 (Sánchez and Perrotti, 2012). This would have direct implications for the liner shipping networks and port infrastructure in the region. If some secondary ports have insufficient handling capacity to accommodate bigger ships, this would support the growth of regional second-tier hubs, which would be able to serve the smaller ports either by smaller feeders or even land transport (thus raising issues relating to the quality and capacity of hinterland infrastructure links).

Ports on the WCSA urgently need to adjust their available draught capacity to 15m and above. In addition, any investment in port superstructure will have to consider a reach for ship-to-shore cranes beyond 50m, as current ships already require more than 45m. The latter factor has special relevance, as crane reach requirements will always have to be met; there is no flexibility as in the case of draught, where a less laden vessel will not require the maximum draught.

The introduction of ever-larger vessels on mainline routes may be attractive for shipping lines but will strain ports severely. Ports invest large sums in upgrading their facilities and competing to receive vessel calls, but handling demand spikes is difficult. Large container drops can result in inefficient crane utilisation as the numerous large cranes required to service large ships are not all required between calls; furthermore, large numbers of containers cannot always be moved in and out of port smoothly. Moreover, shipping lines already have trouble meeting their own schedules; current average reliability across the industry is below 70%. The larger the vessel and the greater the volume of transferred containers at each call, the larger the knock-on effect of poor reliability on the rest of the container system.

A further dimension of technological change driven by the emergence of reefer cargo is discussed below.

Structural change – reefer trade

The global demand for perishable products, especially fruit, has grown substantially, increasing the need for refrigerated seaborne transport capacity. The associated trade flows mainly originate in the southern hemisphere and are directed towards the industrialised countries in the northern hemisphere. In 2010, total seaborne reefer trade was 86.1 million tons, and is expected to reach 112.0 million tonnes by 2016 (Drewry, 2011). WCSA countries exported 14.2 million tonnes of perishable products valued at almost USD 15 billion in 2010, which amounted to 6% of overall export volume (tonnes) and 9% of the sub region's total export value (Vagle, 2012, based on BADECEL, 2012). After Ecuador, Chile is the region's largest exporter of perishables in terms of volume, at 4.8 million tonnes. In 2010, the country's export value of perishables was equivalent to 55% of the whole sub region's export value, reaching almost USD 7.6 billion, making Chile the largest exporter of perishables in terms of value. The average annual growth rate between 1995 and 2010 was 8% in terms of export value, or twice the rate for export volume (4%).

Figure 3.8. **West Coast South America reefer export evolution** (1995-2011)

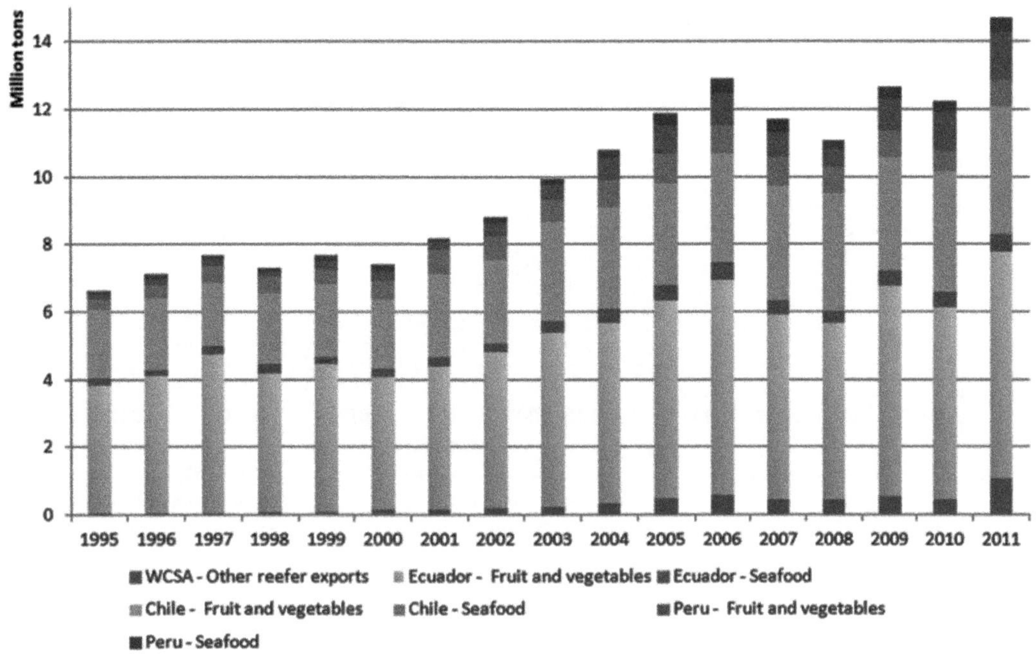

Source: Vagle (2012), based on BADECEL (2012).

The expansion of reefer trade has had important repercussions on the type of vessels deployed in the region, particularly as the transport of reefer cargo has been shifting away from conventional reefer ships to being containerised. For example, between Chile and Northern Europe the share of containerised reefer transport increased from less than 10% in 2000 to over 65% in 2011.

The deployed weekly capacity of TEU and reefer plugs on the WCSA more than trebled on the sub region's main routes. The WCSA-Europe route showed the highest share of reefer slots in relation to TEU capacity, 20% in 2012. On the WCSA-North America and WCSA-Asia routes the share of reefer slots was around 12%. The average number of reefer plugs per string in June 2011 was 364.

This shift is also reflected in the number of reefer slots in the ships deployed in the sub region – up to 1 400 per vessel. The WCSA and the ECSA are the regions where ships with the highest number of reefer plugs are being deployed.

Figure 3.9. **Reefer capacity of vessels deployed on WCSA main routes** (2000-12)

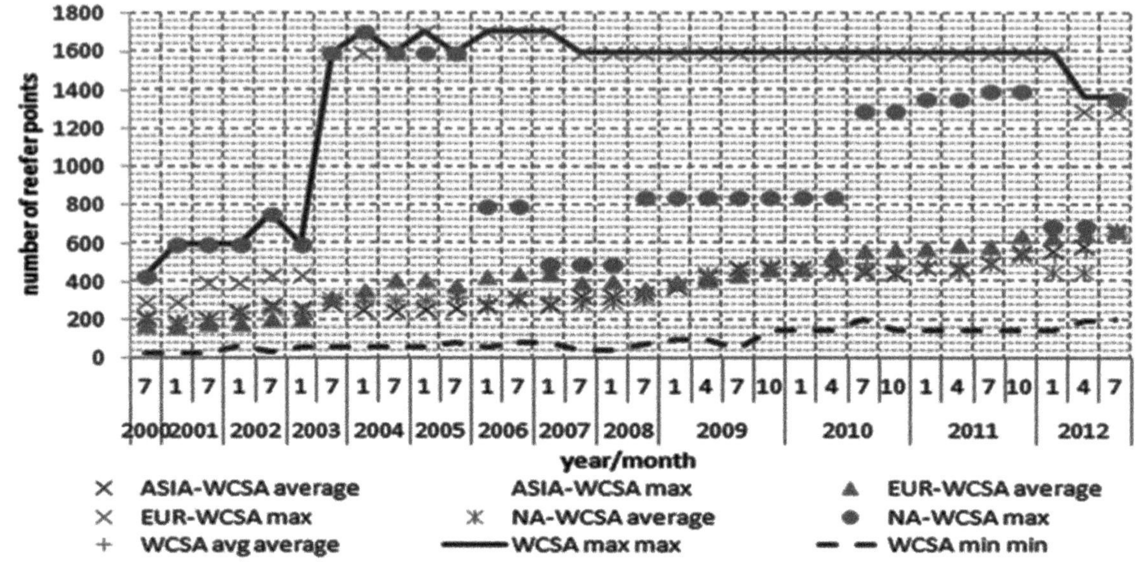

Note: The main trade routes are transpacific, transatlantic and Europe-Asia.
Source: Based on ComPairData, Lloyds List and Marine Traffic, various years.

This structural change in trade also has significant repercussions on ports, as the handling of reefer cargo requires additional installations for cooling and specific services to manage the units. Chile handled around half a million TEU reefer containers in 2012.

Market structure

From the liner shipping perspective, the region and Chile face the challenges of market concentration and the further evolution of liner shipping networks towards hierarchical networks driven by hub-and-spoke strategies, and they are already affected by the repercussions of the cascading effect in ship deployment, which has led to exponential and accelerated growth of ship sizes deployed in the region.

Nominal capacity in 2012 on the WCSA main routes was 54 000 TEU, an increase of 70% from 2009. The WCSA-North America route experienced the greatest increase (130%) over the period, while capacity on the WCSA-Asia route expanded by over 75%.

Figure 3.10. **Evolution of weekly capacity supply on WCSA main routes** (2009-12)

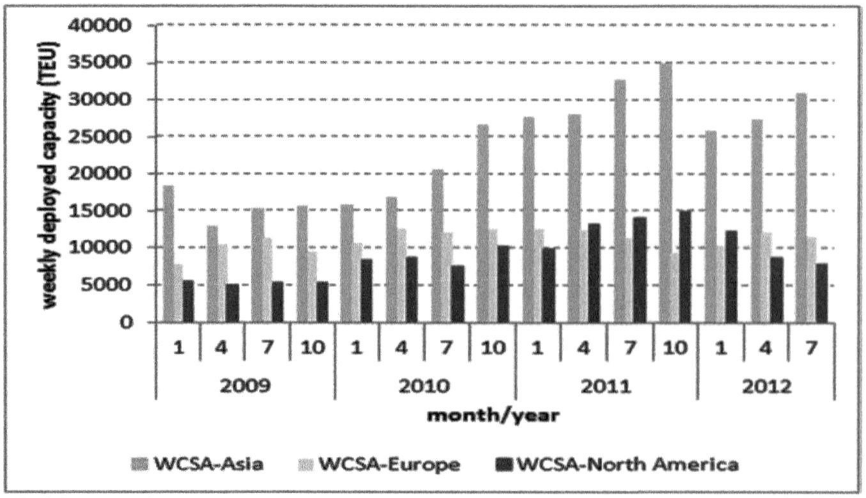

Source: Based on ComPairData, various years.

Nominal capacity increased significantly faster than weekly capacity. The strongest increase in nominal capacity can be observed on the WCSA-Asia services, where it more than doubled between 2008 and 2012. Between 2000 and 2012, nominal deployed capacity on the three main routes (WCSA-Asia, WCSA-Europe and WCSA-North America) quintupled. The differences in nominal capacity are an indicator for the use of slow steaming on the routes, particularly those to Asia and North America.

Beyond capacity, market structure is of high importance to understand potential strategies. In line with Wilmsmeier and Notteboom (2011), a phase of penetration, consolidation and concentration can be observed between 2000 and 2012. At the beginning of the millennium, new operators appeared on the WCSA liner shipping routes (e.g. MSC on the WCSA-Europe route in 2004). Additionally, mergers and acquisitions in the maritime industry had repercussions on the presence of operators in the sub region (notably the takeover of PONL by Maersk). As a result of the crisis, the pattern changed and co-operation between shipping lines, in terms of slot share agreements and jointly operated services, increased. This led to significant movements in the market, as Figure 11 shows for the case of the WCSA-Asia routes. It can be seen that the changes in co-operation and entering and exiting actors particularly increased between April 2010 and January 2012, leading to a period of apparent instability. A result of this period was a significant increase in active operators on the route. However, this was accompanied by a decreasing number of actual services offered.

Figure 3.11. **WCSA-Asia changes in market structure** (2000-12)

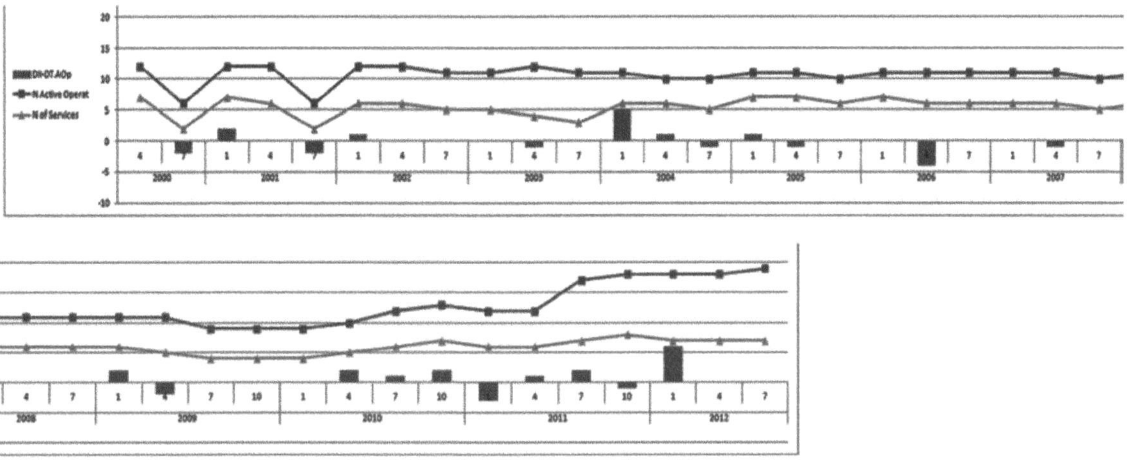

Source: Wilmsmeier and Parushev (2013).

This new form of co-operation also raises questions on the level of competition in the market. Emerging markets such as the WCSA offer a unique opportunity to investigate the behaviour and effectiveness of potential collusive behaviour and pricing. The latter might reduce the competiveness of a country in external trade.

Figure 12, for example, depicts the challenges for the WCSA-Asia route. As the figure shows, five groups compete in this market, despite the fact that more 20 shipping lines are active in the market. Further collaboration between shipping lines carries a risk of quasi-monopolistic markets with potential for collusive behaviour, as is already the case on the WCSA-Europe route.

Figure 3.12. **Market share in nominal TEU capacity by service, WCSA- Asia** (2000-12)

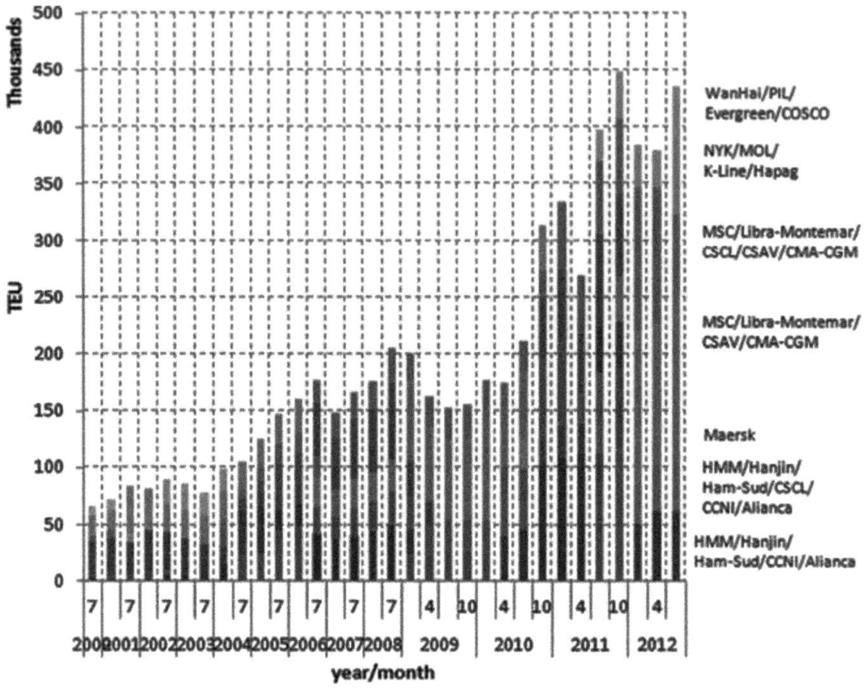

Source: Wilmsmeier and Parushev (2013).

Developments in the liner shipping market have high relevance for future port development, as vertical integration in the market is advancing and thus future port concessions and terminals can result in changes in the competitive environment of the shipping market if a new terminal/port is controlled by a particular group.

Conclusions and outlook

Port infrastructure in its own right as well as the regional and national port system in Chile are at a crossroads, driven by changes in the maritime liner shipping industry, structural transformation and geographical shifts in trade. Traditional port-focused infrastructure development needs to be extended to include the hinterland, and future port system development will have to reach beyond the established centralist vision. Further, current and future changes in the maritime industry will have to be taken into consideration in long term development strategies.

These shifts entail changes beyond physical development, including at main ports, which require solutions that allow future flexibility. Successful port adaptation to infrastructure development in an increasingly competitive environment can only be achieved if institutions and private sector actors are able to act jointly in critical moments and base their action on integrated visions.

References

BADECEL 2012, Base de Datos Estadísticos de Comercio Exterior, Economic Commission for Latin America and the Caribbean (ECLAC) [March, 2012], http://websie.eclac.cl/badecel/badecel_new/bas

Cullinane, K.P.B. and G. Wilmsmeier, 2011, "The contribution of the dry port concept to the extension of port life cycles", in Böse, J.W. (ed), Handbook of Terminal Planning, Springer, New York.

Fleming, D. K., Hayuth, Y., 1994, Spatial characteristics of transportation hubs: centrality and intermediacy. Journal of Transport Geography, 2, 3–18.

Sánchez, R.J. and D. Perrotti, 2012, "Looking into the future: big full containerships and their arrival to South American ports", Maritime policy and Management, Vol. 39, No. 6, pp. 571-88.

Swyngedouw, E. 1992. Territorial organization and the space/technology nexus. Transactions of the Institute of British Geographers, 17: 417–433.

Vagle, R. 2012, Maritime Reefer Trade in West Coast South America: The case of fruits. Maritime Bulletin (50), October, <http://www.cepal.org/id.asp?id=48153>

Wilmsmeier, G., J. Monios and G. Perez, 2013, "Port System evolution: the case of Latin America and the Caribbean", paper presented at IAME Annual Conference, Marseille, July 3-5.

Wilmsmeier, G. and T. Notteboom, 2011 "Determinants of Liner Shipping Network Configuration: A Two Region Comparison, GeoJournal, 76 (3), pp 213-228.

Wilmsmeier, G. and Parushev, T. 2013 Liner shipping industry – evolution, stability and concentration in South American markets. ECLAC. Working paper.

Chapter 4

Efficient hinterland transport infrastructure and services for large container ports

Michele Acciaro, Alan McKinnon[1]

The growth in container volumes and the concentration of container flows on a limited number of hubs, which derives, among other things, from the increasing vessel size, requires the development of new terminal infrastructure at ports able to handle the latest generation of vessels. In addition to the pressure that such vessels impose on the terminal cargo handling capabilities, it is often forgotten, that those larger vessels will also require higher capacity in hinterland transportation or a rationalisation and better use of existing transport alternatives.

This paper provides an overview of the state of the art in hinterland transport management, focusing on the challenges that the development of new container terminal infrastructure is likely to bring to the local communities. Recommendation and a set of good practice case studies are also provided.

1. The Kühne Logistics University, Hamburg, Germany

Introduction

The critical role that container infrastructure plays in favouring the economic development of a country or region is well established. Infrastructure is the necessary condition for efficient cargo handling operations and adequate infrastructure is needed to avoid congestion, foster trade development as well as securing deep-sea container connectivity for economies heavily dependent on international trade. Container infrastructure, however, needs to be complemented by efficient hinterland transport connections if the port is to fully exploit its potential as growth catalyst and supply chain node (Suykens and van de Voorde 1998). Lamentably, it is not uncommon for development projects to focus exclusively on enhancing the infrastructural capabilities of the port, without adequate consideration of the hinterland connections.

The urgency of looking at port and terminal development in conjunction to their hinterland connectivity is exacerbated by the pressure on container terminals to increase their performance levels resulting from the rapid growth of containerised cargo traffic flows and their increased variability. As port capacity cannot be developed as rapidly as increases in demand (Haralambides 2002), any overcapacity is eventually exhausted and episodes of congestion ensue even in the most efficient terminals. This calls for a phased but continuous and well-coordinated effort in expanding container capacity at terminals. Terminal expansions, however, are not always matched by the expansion of hinterland connections.

Terminal operations are affected not only by the larger number of vessel calls but also by the increased variability of call sizes. As Vessels of over 15 000 TEU are becoming increasingly common, despite the fact that they may only be able to access a few large hubs (Cullinane and Khanna 1999). This will concentrate container flows on a few mega-ports, in turn impacting berth and crane productivity of the terminal and adding pressure on hinterland links, often with adverse effects on congestion and the environment (Yap and Lam 2013).

The expected increase in transhipment associated with larger vessel size, is likely to impact on the terminals not only forcing them to handle higher volumes in the same period of time, but also to reduce the variability of their operations (i.e. increase reliability) in order to guarantee seamless flows of cargo among transhipment ports and/or transhipment port and feeder ports (Gilman 1999). The increases in productivity and reliability at terminals will require more tracking, greater container visibility and more emphasis on environmental and regulatory compliance particularly as terminals now occupy critical positions the supply chain (Notteboom 2008).

Terminals are increasingly requested to act as buffers and accommodate the requests of their clients (i.e. primarily the shipping lines) concerning last minute schedule changes, delays, break of calls, yard storage, etc. (Notteboom 2006). All these changes take place against the background of ever increasing competition among terminals (Heaver, Meersman and van de Voorde 2001). As logistics and hinterland transportation develop further, shipping lines may become less committed to certain terminals and instead try to secure capacity in various terminals to be able to maintain flexibility. Inefficient terminals rapidly lose their competitive edge, as slow turnaround times result in higher inventory costs and have negative repercussions for the entire supply chain (Heaver 2002).

The development of supply chain networks imposes a set of challenges for ports and terminal operators (Notteboom 2008, Heaver, Meersman and van de Voorde 2001, Song 2003). Supply chain management in fact becomes an integral part of port management, and therefore it becomes increasingly important to assess priorities in the management of container terminal process effectiveness (Brooks and

Schellinck 2013). The cost reductions derived from moving production processes to low cost locations can only be enjoyed as long as the supply chains supporting these processes work. It should be stressed that logistics not only supports modern production process but it enriches them by delivering added value (Lee, Nam and Song 2012).

The major difficulty with this approach though is related to the fact that the terminal is only one of the agents involved in the supply chain (Notteboom 2008). As such its ability to create added value is constrained by the actions of the other agents in the supply chain, whether they are the shipping line, the trucking companies, the hinterland operators, the port authority or the distribution centres where the containers will be ultimately delivered (Fransoo and Lee 2012).

In recent years, the importance of framing terminals and ports in the supply chain perspective has become evident (Song and Panayides 2008). Shippers and consignees increasingly require the responsibility for all logistic activities to be assumed by global supply chain specialists and logistics integration has become a common strategy of transport providers (Frankel 1999). Robinson (2002) argues that this new paradigm ports and terminals being components of global supply chains, although enticing, is still relatively uncommon (Song and Panayides 2008, Tongzon, Chang and Lee 2009). Although ports clearly have a role to play in global supply chains, they are often unable to influence or affect chain competitiveness beyond their own boundaries (Carbone and de Martino 2003).

The development and expansion of container ports therefore needs to be supported by good hinterland transportation and adequate provisions must be made for rail or road capacity if the container terminal has to function and add value. Typically the port hinterland logistics chain processes can be segmented in terminal gate processes, the hinterland transport processes and dry ports. Hinterland transport should be divided into road, rail and inland waterways. Considering that with some noticeable exceptions, inland waterways play a limited role in most ports, less attention has been devoted to this mode (e.g. Wiegmans et al. 2004, Konings 2007, Notteboom 2007).

Each of these hinterland logistics chain components plays a critical role in ensuring that the terminal delivers its supply chain value. Hinterland chain coordination has become an even more significant attribute of the effectiveness of container terminals as social and environmental sustainability considerations are taken into account. It is only through terminal and hinterland coordination that some of the negative externalities associated with large container ports can be managed, as the success of the dry port concept seems to attest. Terminal managers, public authorities and logistics service providers need therefore to embed the sustainability of the container hinterland process in the terminal expansion and development plans. These processes start at the terminal gate, and include inland transport to a dry port and beyond. The rest of the paper will focus on each of the hinterland chain components, highlighting their relations with each other and with the terminal. Particular attention is paid to the role that coordination plays in these processes and what strategies can be adopted to reduce the carbon footprint of the hinterland transport chain.

Port gate management

The role of gate management

Container terminals are transmodal facilities whose efficiency is dependent on the execution of distinct but interconnected processes. Typically container terminal processes are subdivided into three main groups: waterside, yard and landside (Stahlbock and Voß 2008). While it is not unusual for container terminals to perform deep-sea or feeder transhipment operations, most terminals have at least a small percentage of gateway traffic, i.e. containers that are transloaded from container ships through the yard and eventually to some mode of land transport and *vice versa*.

The intensity and complexity of landside activities vary considerably depending on the size of the terminal, the type of transportation infrastructure available in the region and the operations technologies used on the terminal. Larger terminals tend to rely on a mix of rail, road, and, when available, barge transportation to the hinterland. Road transport, however, is most often the main hinterland transportation modes in view of its flexibility and the possibly of trucks going virtually wherever there is a road (Veenstra, Zuidwijk and van Asperen 2012).

The port gates are one of the most critical pieces of terminal infrastructure where a large part of technical and administrative procedures take place. In addition to separating and protecting the terminal from the outside, terminal gates also act as administrative border for custom and other legal procedures and function as the interface between the terminal and the hinterland. Since the overall efficiency of a terminal is dependent on the efficiency of its subsystems, terminals are particularly wary of delays at a gate (Zhao and Goodchild 2010). Gate operations are often the result of a coordination effort between the terminal and shippers, drayage and rail operators, freight forwarders and port authorities (Giuliano and O'Brien 2008, Chen, Govindan and Yang 2013).

For this reason the efficiency of gate operations has been investigated extensively, especially in relation to trucking operations, in the attempt to improve their performance, eliminate congestion and bottlenecks or reduce negative environmental externalities. Gate systems can be grouped in three major types: 'first come first serve', appointment systems and time window systems (Giuliano and O'Brien 2007, Chen, Govindan and Yang 2013). Most terminals use a 'first come first serve' policy, where container trucks are loaded or unloaded depending on their arrival time at the terminals. One of the major disadvantages of such method is that it often generates peaks in operations and queuing ensues (Chen, Govindan and Yang 2013).

Terminal operators have attempted to enforce appointment systems, either offering the possibility of making an appointment, or providing penalties for operators that do not appear at the terminals at the right time(Huynh 2009, Guan and Liu 2009). While the advantages of an appointment system are easily comprehensible, its implementation in practice has been met often with scepticism. This is partly because the effectiveness of an appointment system depends on the opening hours of distribution facilities and warehouses, and to some extent on labour and road regulation (Giuliano and O'Brien 2007). The implementation of appointment systems has been often driven more by the regulator than by the industry, leading some to argue that industry self-regulation would have delivered better results (e.g. in California, see Giuliano and O'Brien 2007). In some cases, such as in the case of Southampton discussed below and other British ports, however, the implementation of an appointment system has brought visible benefits in terms of emission and congestion reduction (Morais and Lord 2006). This has led other ports around the world, such as Port Metro Vancouver in Canada and port Botany in Australia, to implement similar appointment systems (Davies 2013).

An alternative is offered by time windows systems, which have been used mostly at container terminal facilities in China (Chen, Govindan and Yang 2013, Chen and Yang 2010). The system allows a better coordination of terminal operation, aligned with vessel arrivals, and overall would improve terminal utilisation. The terminal informs freight forwarders of a vessel arrival and allocates a time window for trucking operations. This appointment system reduces the time containers station at the terminal and allows for better loading, as the containers are more easily identified and located at the terminal. In practice however, it appears that the system has not been able to eliminate idle time for truck operators outside the terminals (Chen, Govindan and Yang 2013).

The extended gate concept

In order to resolve the complexities associated with terminal gate management and to reduce congestion in the proximity of the port, the extended gate concept has been proposed as an alternative to direct trucking operations at the port (Veenstra, Zuidwijk & van Asperen 2012). The extended gateway would allow truck operators to move containers to a hinterland location, ideally making use of barge or rail connection. In this way the terminal can reduce congestion at its gates as well as reducing pressure on its yard capacity. The concept has been associated with that of dry ports (e.g. Roso, Woxenius & Lumsden 2009a, Bergqvist, Wilmsmeier & Cullinane 2013a), which will be discussed more in detail later.

At the basis of the dry-port concept is the ability to relocate some loading and unloading operations inland in order to exploit economies of scale from route density and reducing external costs (see for example Bergqvist 2012). Dry ports allow concentrating cargo on barge or rail trunk links, eventually ensuring better capacity utilisation the lower per unit cost. In this way modal shift from road to rail or barge becomes economically attractive. In addition road traffic in congested port areas is reduced and trucks do not need to transit through the metropolitan areas in the vicinity of the port. As already highlighted by Rodrigue (1999), among others, synchronisation of container terminal activities across the supply chain allows terminals to increase their competitive advantage. The extended gate concept then is based on the possibility for the terminal to perform its gate activities at the inland terminal. Transportation to the inland terminal is then internalised by the terminal operator, which is in a position to move large volumes by rail or barge inland (Veenstra, Zuidwijk and van Asperen 2012).

Some of the issues associated with the extended gate concept are related to the terminal location decision the coordination of container movements (e.g. different containers arrive and are requested by their customers at different times), the connectivity of rail or barge transport, information exchange, network design and administrative (e.g. customs) procedures. The growth of vessel sizes, as outlined in the introduction, requires container terminals to find alternative and more innovative ways to handle container flows at the terminal gate and the extended gateway could provide a valuable option.

Practical considerations

The efficiency and effectiveness of a gate operation system depends on the availability and characteristics of IT systems employed at the terminal, the degree of coordination and information exchange among operators, labour regulation, safety and security policy at a terminal level as well as truck labour regulation. It is expedient to focus on three main practical considerations that might affect the efficacy of specific gate management systems:

i) *IT infrastructure*. there is the need to provide accurate and on time information. Data exchange is instrumental not only for allowing coordination among hinterland transport actors, but also to ensure visibility in the chain for efficiency, security and planning purposes. As highlighted by Kia et al. (2000), among others, the role of ICT in terminal management is critical to ensure efficient operations. Gate systems typically operate as part of a multipoint system, where information on the container manifest, the cargo or the truck driver can be collected and linked to the terminal EDI system (Guan and Liu 2009, Huynh 2009, Zhao and Goodchild 2010). Increasingly container terminals make use of advanced identification technologies for security and efficiency reasons (Marchet, Perotti and Mangiaracina 2012, Shi, Tao & Voß 2011, Hu et al. 2011), and these are an essential component for integration along the supply chains (Song and Panayides 2008, Marchet, Perotti and Mangiaracina 2012, Almotairi and Lumsden 2009). Challenges on the implementation of ICT at terminals and ports are well documented also in developed markets (Helling and Poister 2000), and cooperation or joint ventures between terminal operators and transport service providers have been able to improve terminal gate systems through ICT innovation (Bagchi and Paik 2001).

ii) *labour regulation and trucking industry practices.* The implementation of a gate appointments system that might appear a feasible way to improve container terminal gate efficiency often faces challenges related to labour regulation, working practices in the industry and inherent difficulties in managing the process (Goel and Kok 2012a, Goel and Kok 2012b). The applications of a gate appointments scheme appear to have been more successful when there has been a stronger action from the side of the regulator (Giuliano and O'Brien 2008, van Asperen, Borgman and Dekker 2011), but in general, with a few exceptions, have not delivered the expected benefits (van Asperen, Borgman and Dekker 2011). Labour regulation and industry practices, such as opening hours of distribution facilities and customer warehousing, remain a critical factor for the efficiency of gate systems.

iii) *security and custom procedures at the terminal.* Security and custom regulation can impose substantial delays in the operation of the terminal and it is therefore vital that coordination with the agencies responsible for these activities is negotiated and security practices are embedded in terminal gate management. Literature now exists in the area of security for container logistics (Acciaro and Serra 2013), but major issues remain with reference to the impact of scanning procedures (Bakshi, Flynn and Gans 2011), ISPS code (Yang 2010, Lirn and Wang 2010) or terminal operation resilience (Lewis, Erera and White 2003, Yeo, Pak and Yang 2013). From the analysis of 470 container terminals it appears that security has a negative impact on the operational efficiency of terminals, especially through inspection regimes, although the nature and scale of this impact depends substantially on the type of regulation and security strategy of the terminal (Bichou 2011).

Case study: The container terminal appointment system in the port of Southampton

The port of Southampton is the second largest container port in the UK after Felixstowe. It has a single container terminal, DP World Southampton, which handled 1.6 million TEU in 2012. The terminal experienced yard congestion and delays in truck turn-around times between 2001 and 2004, mostly as a result of peaks in truck arrivals and the rapid growth in container volumes. The terminal implemented in 2003 a voluntary scheme that would allow trucks to book their time slots. The scheme did not appear to be successful and in 2005 a new mandatory vehicle booking system was implemented (Davies 2013).

The new system regulates truck access to the terminal by limiting the maximum number of booking per hour to 10% of the total number of appointments. Appointment bookings if planned during peak-hours cost £1 while they are free for off-peak hours. The terminal also charges a no show fee of £25. Bookings can modified free of charge, they can be moved as long as there is available capacity and the 10% maximum has not been reached and if not needed can be returned to an exchange where they can be taken up by another carrier.

The system, which has been improved in 2013 with the introduction of a new visual interface, has been successful in reducing turn-around times for trucks and other terminals in Tilbury and Felixstowe have implemented similar systems. The features that appear to make it a particularly usable and effective system relate to its flexibility and user friendliness (Davies 2013).

Road investment and congestion management

Hinterland Logistics and Infrastructure Development.

Of the various factors influencing the competitiveness of a port, the quality of transport infrastructure across its hinterland is one of the most critical (ITF, 2008). There have been numerous examples of new port developments under-performing because of a lack of investment in supporting transport infrastructure. This is hardly surprising as good hinterland connectivity is one of the key criteria that shipping lines, shippers and logistics service providers take into accounting in deciding on their choice of port (Wiegmans et al, 2008). This connectivity can be measured in several ways, by the:

- density of inland transport networks
- accessibility to key industrial and logistical centres – measured by transit time and transport costs
- range of modal options available to carriers
- capacity of the main corridors
- reliability of deliveries across the hinterland

These aspects of connectivity are clearly inter-related. Inadequate capacity, for example, causes congestion which in turn impairs reliability. This inter-relationship between capacity, congestion and reliability is fundamental to the planning of hinterland transport networks. It has become increasingly important as a result of six major trends:

a) The tightening of logistical schedules as companies have cut inventory levels and compressed order cycle times. This has made their production and distribution systems more vulnerable to delays at a time when globalisation has extended their supply lines and made them more dependent on deep-sea container services.

b) The rapid growth in container traffic that has occurred mainly as result of trade liberalisation and the globalisation of manufacturing and procurement strategies.

c) The sharp increase in the size of container vessels which is causing inland flows to spike and create bottlenecks at weak links on hinterland networks.

d) The concentration of production capacity and inventory in fewer locations as companies seek economies of scale. This is consolidating container flows on key corridors, which often lack the capacity to cope.

e) The adoption of 'slow steaming' by container shipping lines, primarily to cut bunker fuel costs. To compensate for the lengthening of transit-times on the maritime leg, shippers are keen to accelerate hinterland transport and improve its reliability to minimise adverse effects on production and distribution schedules (Maloni et al., 2013).

f) The shift in the balance of costs between deep-sea and hinterland transport. As increasing vessel size reduces cost per TEU-km on the maritime leg, the share of total door-to-door costs attributable to hinterland transport increases (Notteboom 2008). The share is further inflated by rising energy prices (as the energy-intensity of hinterland transport is significantly higher than of deep-sea shipping) and deteriorating reliability on congested hinterland networks.

These trends emphasise the importance of logistics to the planning of hinterland transport, a subject that has attracted significant academic attention over the past decade (e.g. Notteboom and Rodrigue 2007, 2008). Much has been written about the transformation of ports from basic transport terminals to supply chain hubs in an effort to extend their range of value-adding services (e.g. Carbone and de Martino 2003). In pursuit of added value shipping lines have also diversified into land-based logistics. Another aspect of this 'logistification' of maritime transport, which has so far generated less interest, is the alignment of hinterland infrastructure planning with the changing geography of companies' logistics systems (McKinnon 2010). In many countries the interface between the container shipping network and shippers' supply chains has been changing, altering the pattern of container movement within national markets. As Hall and Jacobs (2010) argue, keeping ports competitive in this new regime requires 'coordinated action, both within existing supply chains and between competing supply chains that share the same port–hinterland spaces and infrastructure' (p.1113).The state clearly has a role to play in relieving congestion on major routes to the ports. It is common for local and central government to shoulder this burden of infrastructural improvement. In the UK, governments have required port developers to invest in link roads in the vicinity of the port to facilitate access and avert potential congestion problems. Governments can also influence congestion levels and patterns of traffic flow, while raising revenue for infrastructural improvement across port hinterlands, by imposing tolls on truck movement (McKinnon, 2006).

The pattern of container movement is largely shaped by the locations at which containers are loaded and unloaded (so-called 'transloading' locations) and the repositioning of empty containers within the hinterland either to collect an export consignment or to be returned to a port for global redistribution.

Location of transloading facilities

The very essence of containerisation is to allow goods to move in sealed, standardised modules on a door-to-door basis. The location of these 'doors' is changing, however, as companies modify the points in their supply chains at which the containerisation and 'de-containerisation' operations occur. Recent research in the UK has found that the vast majority of inbound containers are bound for general distribution centres (DCs) or dedicated DCs for imported goods, located at strategic locations for national and regional distribution within the country. Deviations from this pattern are beginning to emerge, however. For example:

i) Port-centric logistics: this concept applies mainly, though not exclusively, to inbound container traffic and involves 'destuffing' the container at a DC in the vicinity of the port (Mangan et al. 2008). The imported goods are stored and handled there and subsequently distributed in conventional trucks or rail wagons to customers across the hinterland. PCL has been heavily promoted in recent years by port authorities and property developers, particularly in the UK and US, and is well-exemplified by the new $2 bn London Gateway port developed by DP World in the Thames estuary. When fully developed, this port will combine a six-berth container terminal and adjoining 450 hectare distribution park.

PCL confers advantages for port authorities, shipping lines and shippers. For port authorities it offers a means of exploiting unused land, diversifying into value-adding logistics services and securing greater shipper loyalty. Shipping lines can accelerate container turnaround times and, in the case of countries with unbalanced container flows, minimise empty container movement across the hinterland. Shippers can distribute their products more directly from port-based DCs, eliminating links in the supply chain, reducing inland transit times and sometimes taking advantage of lower cost land. Against these advantages, however, shippers must weigh the disadvantages of siting a DC in a location peripheral to the national market and making a long-term commitment to a particular port's portfolio of container services. Peripherality will be less of a problem where the port is located close to a major concentration in population / industry, as in the case of London Gateway, and where most, if not all, of the products stored and handled by the port-based DC pass through the port. Where the DC also draws products from many other sources a port-based location may be sub-optimal relative to a more centrally-located facility (Monios and Wilmsmeier 2012).

Wide adoption of the PCL model would have significant implications for transport infrastructure development. The clustering at a port of DCs providing radial distribution across a national market would require good multi-directional road, and possibly rail, access. Unlike the traditional hinterland movement of containers to inland terminals and dry ports, which involves channelling container flows along strategic corridors to major hubs, deliveries from DCs are typically much more dispersed to final points of sale and use. The transloading of freight from containers to articulated trucks also tends to increase total cube, partly because of the greater use of unitised handling equipment in land-based logistics but also because the density with which products are packed into deep-sea containers is generally higher than that on surface transport. It can therefore require several trucks to distribute a single container-load of densely-packaged imports (McKinnon 2013).

PCL also has implications for freight modal split in the port hinterland. For example, the replacement of container flows with the movement of freight emerging from port-based DCs in loose or palletised form can make it more difficult for rail to compete. The greater dispersal of hinterland deliveries from these DCs can also make it difficult for rail freight operators to consolidate flows into viable train-loads, particularly within the tight delivery schedules imposed on wholesale and retail supply chains downstream of the port. In most countries, the railways command a smaller share of freight movement at the 'secondary distribution' level outbound from DCs than at the primary level feeding product into factories and DCs. All of this suggests that PCL may tilt the hinterland mode split in favour of road, though this has still to be confirmed empirically.

ii) Consolidation of container loads: another logistical trend which is evident in both exporting and receiving markets is the channelling of maritime freight through inland consolidation centres to improve levels of container fill and increase opportunities for the back-loading of containers. Major retailers sourcing products from numerous suppliers in a given market are increasingly consolidating less-than-container loads (LCL) at hub locations. Similarly, manufacturers with numerous production and warehouses sites, from which container flows were traditionally uncoordinated, are now establishing hubs through which deep-sea freight can be bundled into more viably-sized container loads. This yields a net reduction in ocean freight costs despite the fact it adds an extra node and link to the maritime supply chain. It can also increase the opportunities for shifting freight to rail (or inland waterway) by aggregating container flows into train or barge loads. This modal shift effect is reinforced where several companies cluster their 'maritime hubs' at locations with good access to rail and waterway networks.

Repositioning of empty containers

Marshalling the stock of empty containers is one of the greatest challenges of containerisation. In almost every country it is considered very inefficient, though the degree of sub-optimality is very difficult to assess given the lack of data on empty container movements. It is common, for example, for containers emptied at an import location to be returned to the port prior to despatch to an export location to collect its next load. Where 'triangulation' occurs within the hinterland, the routing is often needlessly circuitous. Even where container loads are received and generated by the same factory or warehouse, the chances of an inbound container being reloaded with an export consignment are often quite limited. As a result of these practices:

- Container turnaround times are lengthened.
- Shippers are often unable to get an adequate supply of the specific types and sizes of container they require when they need them.
- Much unnecessary transport is generated across the hinterland, increasing traffic levels, costs and emissions.

Inefficiency in the landward repositioning of empty containers has persisted for a several reasons, including poor IT, the refusal of shipping lines to share boxes, tight demurrage restrictions and a general lack of co-ordination between stakeholders. The concept of the 'grey box' has long been advocated as a means of pooling empty container capacity and thus rationalising the movement of empty containers across hinterlands. There are few examples, however, of it being successfully or sustainably applied. The adoption of PCL would also help to ease the empty repositioning problem, though, as discussed earlier, this may prove to be attractive to limited numbers of companies with specific logistics requirements.

An alternative, or supplementary, option would be to use some of the empty container capacity in the domestic distribution of industrial and retail supplies. This would entail greater integration of maritime and domestic logistics within the port hinterland and some relaxation of current restrictions on the use and return of containers. It could lead to containers being increasingly used to carry domestic loads on routes back to the port or to an export location. In those countries where much of the hinterland movement of containers is handled by merchant haulage, shippers have a strong interest in maximising revenue from container repositioning trips, incentivising them and their carriers to find backloads. Online load matching sites can facilitate the search for suitable backloads, though the deployment of empty container capacity in domestic logistics also requires the adaptation of handling systems and reception bays at industrial and commercial premises. Overall, as in so many aspects of hinterland transport, there would be a need for much greater co-ordination between all the relevant actors to take full advantage of this proposal (van der Horst and de Langen 2008).

Rationalisation of the movement of empty containers across the hinterland would ease infrastructural pressures on key routes to and from the port, particularly where repositioning regularly entails the routing of boxes via the port terminal.

Rail access to terminals

Rail hinterland transport: International experiences

In order to reduce congestion on road transportation and to exploit the economies of traffic density one of the solutions that is most often advocated is to increase the share of rail and inland waterways to that of trucks. These two alternative modes of transport offer substantial cost and environmental advantage, but are generally less flexible and require increased coordination as multiple private operators and public agencies need to cooperate harmoniously. This coordination does not come about spontaneously, but requires specific policy action (van der Horst and de Langen 2008).

Given the complexity of rail coordination, the potential for a switch to rail for transportation to/from container terminals is dependent on the institutional model that is used for rail in a particular country. Railway infrastructure and operational configurations typically are subdivided on the basis of the degree of geographical and functional integration (Pittman 2007). While there are arguments in favour and against various institutional configuration models, in the specific case of railway access to container terminals the development of dedicated freight corridors often requires the agreement of multiple actors, network operators and the infrastructure developer. Furthermore, in case a mixed network, i.e. networks that cater simultaneously for passenger and freight transport, the relations with the passenger rail operator can become a critical factor.

In Europe, policy has aimed at separating infrastructure management from passenger and freight operation, in an attempt to overcome the natural monopoly held by nation-wide integrated rail networks. The transition from national railway monopolies to an integrated network of nationally-managed infrastructure and European-wide rail operators is far from completed. The reform has favoured the development of dedicated railway companies especially in the vicinity of larger ports. The number of container shuttle services has been rising and is expected to increase in response to environmental and economic pressures. In particular the development of dedicated freight corridors, such as the "Betuwe Route" in the Netherlands, with more than 350 trains per week, or the "Iron Rhine" in Belgium, that contributes to the 200 container trains departing from Antwerp weekly, aim at improving the conditions for rail transportation (Meersman et al. 2008).

A particularly successful case relates to the development of hinterland cargo movement by rail from the port of Hamburg and Bremen to their hinterland. In Hamburg the port railways network is managed by the Port Authority and is responsible for the movement of 2 million TEU along the 300 km network (Free and Hanseatic City of Hamburg and Hamburg Port Authority 2012). 92 operators are licenced to use the port rail infrastructure and this accounts for over 30 per cent of Hamburg container flows being handled by rail (against the 10% handled by Rotterdam and Antwerp). Today the port handles approximately 200 trains per day and this is expected to double in the next decade. The port of Bremerhaven has the highest percentage share of container rail transport of all, with over 45% of container throughput being moved inland by rail.

In the case of Russia freight rail transport is currently responsible for the very high utilisation of rail infrastructure (Pittman 2004). The intention behind rail reforms in Russia, and elsewhere, was increasing the sector efficiency and providing competitive options for shippers (Pittman 2013). The advantages of the rail option are well recognised and in order to foster the competitiveness of the new port of Ust Luga, plans exist to develop the hinterland rail infrastructure between the port and the Predportovy Distriport and Interterminal Predportovy, as well as other logistics facilities in the Saint Petersburg area (Korovyakovsky and Panova 2011).

The penetration of rail transportation in Asia has not followed the same pattern around the continent with marked differences between the systems used in China, India and South-East Asia. While rail transportation does not show the same degree of efficiency as in some other parts of the world, intermodality is becoming increasingly important. The development of Chinese dry-ports is still hindered by congested infrastructure and administrative inefficiencies (Beresford et al. 2012). The Indian case is characterised by congestion and a very fragmented logistics infrastructure (Ng and Gujar 2009, Haralambides and Gujar 2011) with virtually no rail transportation in South-East Asia.

In North America, rail transportation has for long constituted the backbone of freight movement and the development of an integrated network of dry ports. In particular, the development of freight hubs, such as Chicago, has been made possible by the affordable and reliable rail freight transport connecting large ports to inland satellite terminals and load centres (Rodrigue et al. 2010). Issues related to capacity constraints and the difficulties in coordinating expansion among the seven main independent rail operators and the transmodal challenges in Chicago, including severe congestion and heightened safety risks, have started to affect the efficiency of the system (Rodrigue and Notteboom 2010).

Following the disruption of the rail system as a result of a snow storm in the winter 1999/2000, the Chicago Region Environmental and Transportation Efficiency Programme (CREATE) was developed as a public private partnership to seek funding for the necessary expansion and maintenance work needed to expedite passenger and freight train movements in the area (Monios and Lambert 2013). The cost of this programme was in the region of US$ 1.5 billion, of which approximately 15% is funded by the railroads, and the rest is financed through various forms of local, state and federal sources (Monios and Lambert 2013).

In the South American railway sector reform has been carried out extensively and completed by the nineties, with Mexico and Argentina leading the way, and Brazil following in more recent times. The system has been characterised by the preference for vertically integrated railroad concessions. The main challenges in those countries for the attractiveness of railway in terms of freight corridors seems to be related to the very high competition among operators and from the road transport sector as well as the management of access rights to the main ports, e.g. traffic to the port of Santos in Brazil had to be interchanged for the last 22 km since the link to the port was privatised (Eustache, Goldstein and Pittman 2001, Padilha and Ng 2012).

Coordination challenges in rail hinterland transport

As shown in the geographical review of the previous section, coordination in hinterland railways does not come about spontaneously, but requires specific policy action. As van den Horst and de Langen (2008) explain, difficulties in coordination emerge as a result of the multiple actors being involved in developing and planning of container rail transport infrastructure.

Van den Horst and de Langen (2008) list some of the coordination problems arising in container rail transport, specifically: unused capacity and congestion, often combined in the peak-load problem, delays due to limited planning on rail terminals, and limited exchange of traction and of rail cargo. They also suggest four major ways in which such coordination can be improved:

- Introduction of incentives: through the development of a reward or penalty systems, differentiated tariffs or capacity auctioning, such as the incentive system developed in Long Beach in 2009/2010 in order to stimulate shipping lines and terminals to move containers by rail.
- Creation of inter-firm alliances: through joint ventures, project specific contracts or other forms of vertical cooperation along the chain e.g. agreement to exchange locomotives among Dutch rail companies.
- Organisation scope change: introduction of mechanisms for risk sharing or integration along the chain, the development of Rail4Chem (now part of SNCF), the European Bulls Rail Freight Alliance, or the SHIFT2RAIL initiative, aiming at developing interoperable rail technologies and favour modal shift.
- Collective action: through governmental intervention or private intervention, e.g. development of user platforms for rail cargo exchanges and rail freight promotion initiatives, such as Port of Hamburg 62+, aiming at stimulating modal shift for cargo to Bavaria.

Value adding through container rail transport at ports

In order to understand the challenges associated with the use of container terminal transportation by rail to and from the hinterland of a port, it is important to distinguish between three interlinked but distinct issues:

i) *Value for the users.* Container rail transportation will be valuable as long as shippers can gain some form of benefit from using rail transport. In recent years the question of the competitiveness of intermodal chains has emerged. In addition to clear environmental benefits that can be obtained from using rail transportation, the question remains about whether reliability and cost savings can compensate for the greater flexibility offered by road transportation.

ii) *Rail service quality and price.* The attractiveness of the rail link depends on the pricing policies, the quality of the service and the conditions under which the rail connection is provided. Pricing policies for rail connections are difficult to formulate and typically do not allow for full infrastructural cost recovery. The efficiency of the network, access to terminals and shunting yards, and the interaction with other parts of the network are also likely to influence the reliability and effectiveness of rail transport. In particular marshalling and switching infrastructure, signalling and the degree and availability of electrified tracks and terminals are some of the aspects to be considered to assess the attractiveness of the rail and rail terminal facilities.

iii) *Rail network development and financing.* Given the costs associated with the development of railroad infrastructure, the model employed to build and finance the network is also likely to have an impact on operation. While the use of public private partnerships appears quite successful in the development and management of road infrastructure, its implementation in the case of rail or other intermodal infrastructure has been less encouraging. This implies that the development of new freight rail infrastructure typically require a certain degree of public funding. This is particularly true in the case of vertically separated railroad networks. Dedicated rail corridors in areas with predictable and stable volumes might prove more attractive, but typically infrastructure recovery times are longer than what the private sector is willing to accept and, given the economies of scale associated with rail infrastructure development, private financing may result in under-provision or under-maintenance (Monios and Lambert 2013).

Among some interesting cases it might be worth mentioning the Alameda corridor in California. The corridor is a short 20 mile (32 km) high capacity (3 double-stack tracks) railway link between the ports of Los Angeles/Long Beach and the main rail trunk lines of Union Pacific (UP) and Burlington Northern Santa Fe (BNSF) opened in 2002. The total cost of the project was approximately US$ 2.43m half of which funded through revenue bonds and the rest through a mix of federal loans and support by the port authorities.

Case study: Government support for the rail freight sector in the UK

In Great Britain rail freight is carried by private train operators on track owned by a private, 'not for shareholder dividend' infrastructure company. Freight pays track access charges on the basis of avoidable costs. These usually cover only wear and tear and operational management costs. They do not currently reflect capital investment costs as freight is rarely the prime user of rail tracks in the UK, although the rail regulator is considering introducing contributions to capital investment costs for some categories of freight as volumes grow on some routes. Capital investment can therefore be a barrier to expanding rail freight services to ports, although in recent years containerized rail services have benefited from the enlargement of the 'loading gauge' on strategic routes to the main deep-sea ports of Southampton and Felixstowe, permitting the movement of 9'6" boxes. The Southampton link was jointly funded by government and industry. The largest share of funding was provided by the Department for Transport (£43m). Other contributors included Associated British Ports, the South East England Development Agency and the European Regional Development Fund. In the year following gauge enhancement on the line from Southampton to the West Coast Main Line, the main spinal rail route in the UK, rail's share of container movements to / from this port rose from 29% to 36% (Freightliner, 2013). The gauge enhancement to Felixstowe was financed out of the Department for Transport's Transport Innovation Fund.

Since 1974 the UK government has operated a Freight Facilities Grant (FFG) Scheme which provides capital support for investment in rail freight facilities where it can be demonstrated that a net environmental benefit will accrue from the use of rail rather than road. This benefit is measured by the number of 'sensitive lorry miles' (SLMs) that can be removed from the roads (Department for Transport, 2009a). Different monetary values are assigned to SLMs run on different classes of road, reflecting variations in their environmental sensitivity. The total value of the SLMs saved determines the maximum FFG that can be awarded and hence the extent to which modal shift can be incentivised. Between 1997 and 2011, a total of 45 freight facilities grants (FFGs) were awarded in Scotland with a total value of £62 million, estimated to have removed 34.2 million lorry-miles per annum from Scottish roads and valuing the average SLM at £1.82 (Scottish Government, 2012). Container ports and inland container terminals have been recipients of FFGs and this has improved the relative competitiveness of containerised rail services in port hinterlands.

In 2007, the UK government supplemented the FFG scheme with a Rail Environmental Benefit Procurement Scheme (REPS) which was more targeted on the movement of containers by rail to and from ports over distances of up to 250 miles. REPS provided revenue support, in contrast to the FFG scheme which awarded only capital grants. On a budget of just under £2 million, REPS removed around 120 000 lorry journeys from UK roads over the period 2008-2010. The REPS scheme was discontinued in 2010 and replaced by a Mode Shift Revenue Support (MSRS) Scheme. This new Scheme can effectively subsidise, again for environmental reasons, 'a service conveying deep-sea containers from a port to customers in an inland city' (Department for Transport, 2009b). As in the case of the FFG Scheme, 'a traffic flow is entitled to support if the environmental benefits justify it and the cost of using rail is greater than the cost of road, highlighting a financial need'. It is possible for companies to apply for both FFG and MSRS support, though the environmental benefits are only counted once in the application process. The maximum rate of MSRS support is calculated on a zonal basis, with the UK divided into 18 zones for this purpose. In 2010, for example, a container moving by rail between Thamesport (Zone 18) to Traffic Park near Manchester could be awarded a maximum level of revenue support of £21 (Department for Transport, 2009b).

Dry-ports

Definition

The definition of dry ports is rather ambiguous and has been used to indicate any sort of transmodal facility from simple inland container depots to advanced intermodal distribution and logistics parks. Roso et al. (2009b), define a dry port as an inland intermodal terminal directly connected to seaport(s) by rail where customers can collect or deliver their cargo as if at a seaport. This definition implies, and in this sense is more restrictive than that of intermodal freight terminal advanced for example by UNECE (1998), that there is a conscious and coordinated effort to provide similar services at the dry-port as at the seaport (Roso and Rosa 2012).

The advantages of dry ports stem from their ability to reconfigure inland transport networks improving supply chain performance, boosting local competitiveness and reducing negative externalities (Bergqvist, Wilmsmeier and Cullinane 2013b). One of the key features of dry ports is their intermodal character, as they allow for the exploitation of economies of flow density and the ability to use rail or inland waterway transport. They also act as logistics buffers, in particular in those areas where logistics terminals at ports are required to reduce container dwell times for efficiency reasons or lack of space, such as in the Hamburg-Le Havre port range (Veenstra, Zuidwijk and van Asperen 2012) or in major Chinese ports (Beresford et al. 2012).

The development of inland intermodal terminals is, however, not an effortless endeavour often when their establishment falls under the responsibility of local authorities. In most dry port development experiences there is some form of government intervention, often in partnership with private operators (Bergqvist 2008). The interaction of public and private actors often requires innovative pricing and financial schemes (Monios and Lambert 2013), and may add to the coordination challenges associated with the use of intermodal transport.

Key factors for the development of dry-ports

The development of the dry port has taken different forms globally, and although some general characteristics exist, the local context plays a critical role in the success of a dry port development project (see Bergqvist, Wilmsmeier and Cullinane 2013a for an overview of global experiences). Among the common characteristics at the basis of the successful development of dry ports, Bergqvist (2013) makes the following observations on the basis of a series of research projects:

a) The intermodal facility needs to be developed where there is a market potential. Dry ports with higher profitability tend to be developed faster and put pressure on the public authorities and secure financing.

b) The development of the dry port often requires public support in forms of subsidy and risk mitigation. The different financial perspectives of private and public actors should also be taken into account, as the financiers will have different investment time horizons.

c) It is often instrumental for the success of a dry port to receive the support of local entrepreneur or public official that can ensure momentum in the development of the logistic concept is not lost. Collaboration among logistics and transport service providers, local and national authorities, manufacturing and distribution facilities is important, As with the case of the development of new container terminal infrastructure, political pressure can interfere with the development process, in some cases delaying or hindering the establishment of a dry port. Political pressure derives from the fact that often the catchment area benefiting from a dry port beyond municipal (and in some cases national) borders, therefore triggering, especially in period of political instability, e.g. at election times, conflicts on the location of the dry port. However, as pointed out for ports by Benacchio et al. (2001), the opposite reaction is also possible, with the development of new infrastructure being resisted on environmental or social grounds.

d) The attitude and overall strategy of the local and national administration is also crucial in the success of a dry port development.

e) As highlighted in the previous section the efficiency of the rail (or barge) transport services is critical in establishing and maintaining the competitiveness of the dry port and any connected distribution facility.

f) The operational characteristics of the terminal in terms terminal layout, terminal infrastructure, road configuration, IT and security infrastructure determine the efficiency of terminal operations. For the dry port to achieve its efficiency targets, this infrastructure has to be in place and adequate maintenance provisions need to be made.

g) From a more administrative and organisational perspective newly developed dry ports need to have a clear ownership structure and transparent organisation. This ensures long-term credibility and reduces risk exposure to the users. Such transparency and openness conditions can be stipulated in the contractual agreements governing the public private partnership.

h) The practice of tendering has generated improvements in the level and pace of innovation, but has also required a clearer statement on the expectations of the local authorities, the pricing and leasing policies allowed, contract characteristics and risk sharing agreements.

Custom operations in dry ports

The impact on operations of custom clearance procedures at ports and in transportation is well established (Clark, Dollar and Micco 2004, Haralambides and Londoño-Kent 2004), and one of the main advantages of dry port is the possibility of concentrating custom inspections outside of the seaport terminals (Roso 2008, Roso, Woxenius and Lumsden 2009b). One of the first definitions of dry ports, Inland Clearance Depot, (UNECE 1998) specifically accounted for the provision of customs clearance services. These facilities are defined as inland intermodal terminals dedicated to the handling and storage of goods under custom transit. The typology of operations performed in dry ports differ globally but typically include good clearance for temporary storage for onward transit, export, warehousing or import (Roso and Lumsden 2010).

The provision of custom clearance and quarantine services imposes high security procedures for accessing the dry port, similarly to seaports, and depending on the country may include high fencing, cameras and guards. However the uptake of custom clearance services shows marked differences among countries as insurance policies and customer habit or preference might interfere with the service use. Security issues can also affect the demand for clearance services or the use of the dry port itself.

Little attention has been paid to the link between port and maritime security and the hinterland transportation networks (Schilk et al. 2007). Schilk et al. (2007) highlight how security at a chain level even for European transport requires further improvements and recommend the development of innovative security strategies and concepts combining maritime with hinterland transport to crate seamless security processes.

Case study: The Betuweroute and the Venlo Dry Port in the Netherlands

The majority of container traffic in continental Europe moves through terminals within the so-called Le Havre–Hamburg port range. This area includes some of the most densely populated areas in Europe with a very highly developed logistics infrastructure network connecting some of the most prosperous markets in the world. Because of the high densities of population, economic activity and traffic, ports in the Hamburg-Le Havre range are under constant pressure to reduce congestion and improve the environmental profile of their hinterland infrastructure. At the same time the critical role that these ports play in the European supply chains requires high levels of economic efficiency and service quality.

The Netherlands has been a major gateway to European supply chains for decades, providing highly efficient transportation primarily to the Netherlands, Belgium and Germany. The port of Rotterdam, still the largest in Europe in terms of throughput, has been able to expand its container traffic because of its proximity to many European production and distribution centres and because of its inland waterway connection. The hinterland transport strategy has been reliant on inland waterways and road, and to a lesser extent railway transportation. In an attempt to encourage the modal shift towards rail, the Dutch government proposed the development of a new dedicated rail corridor to Germany already in 1985, but only in the 1990 was the Betuweroute development fully planned. The project resulted in heightened environmental controversies, high costs that doubled, reaching 4.3 billion Euros (almost four times the estimates from the early 1990), resulting in the end in dropping two of the corridors; the original project had three main rail routes (Ham and Koppenjan 2002). An attempt to involve the private sector in the construction of the 160 km of double drack freight failed (Koppenjan and Leijten 2007) and limited progress took place in completing the links on the German side (now scheduled to be completed in 2015). The Betuweroute is an example of the complexity of implementing good rail connection even on routes with high volumes and in countries with extensive logistics expertise and state-of-the-art infrastructure.

The problem of reducing congestion in port areas has been tackled in the Netherlands also applying the dry-port concept in Venlo, almost at the border with Germany. The intention is to shift part of the handling operations from the port areas to the hinterland making use of rail connections (Rodrigue, et al. 2010). The development of the facilities in Venlo is a classic example of a successful cooperation between transport service providers across countries, terminal operators and port authorities, cargo owners and public authorities.

Managing air emissions

Emissions from Deep-sea Container Supply Chains

It is estimated that shipping accounts for around 3% of global greenhouse gas emissions (IMO 2009), with container ships responsible for approximately a third of this total (Buhaug et al. 2009). These figures relate solely to emissions from the vessels and exclude the environmental impact of ports and hinterland transport. On an inter-continental door-to-door container movement, the deep-sea leg is usually the largest contributor to total carbon emissions, though hinterland transport can represent 20-30% of the total depending on the choice of transport mode (Woolford and McKinnon 2011a). Direct emissions from the port are relatively insignificant, typically contributing 1-2% of the total. It would be wrong, however, on the basis of this estimate, to dismiss the contribution that ports can make to environmental improvement in a container supply chain.

Assessing the environmental impact of ports

It is the ships visiting the ports, rather than port activities themselves that are the main sources of pollution and the main concern is over pollution by noxious gases rather than CO_2 emissions. The dirty bunker fuels ships typically burn emit large quantities of sulphur dioxide, nitrogen oxide and particulate matter in the vicinity of the port, exposing population in the surrounding areas to high and unhealthy concentrations of these noxious gases (California Air Resources Board 2006; Berechman and Tseng 2012). As road transport has traditionally used lighter, cleaner fuels and been subject to much stricter emission controls than shipping, a wide gap exists in the tolerated levels of pollution from these two modes. For example, standard bunker fuel contains on average around 27 000 parts per million (ppm) of sulphur by comparison with the 10-15 ppm found in the fuels used by road vehicles in Europe and the US (International Council for Clean Transportation, 2007). Global efforts to reduce levels of maritime pollution, mostly administered by the IMO under its MARPOL programme, have made limited progress over the past few decades, leaving it to ports to take the environmental lead and try to improve air quality for their local populations. They can do this, for example, by requiring vessels to switch to cleaner, lower-sulphur diesel fuels as they approach the port and by providing shore-side electricity to ships when moored by a practice known as 'cold-ironing. By installing 'scrubbers' to capture sulphur emissions some vessels have been able to meet air quality restrictions while continuing to burn bunker fuel. Several Sulphur Emission Control Areas (SECAs) have also been established around world (e.g. on the Californian coast, the Baltic and North Sea) to reduce the permitted level of sulphur emissions in ship exhaust fumes. Modernisation of the fleet with larger, cleaner, more fuel-efficient vessels is also cutting emission levels per TEU or tonne transported, but the longevity and slow replacement rate of ships makes this a relatively slow process.

On the landward side, some ports have introduced 'clean trucking' schemes. The port of Vancouver, for example, has a Truck Licensing Scheme that restricts access to the port to less polluting vehicles (Braathens 2011). Efforts have also been made to reduce the queuing of trucks coming to collect containers, though this has not always translated into emission reductions (Giuliano and O'Brien 2007). Some ports with the necessary infrastructure are promoting a modal shift to rail and waterborne transport. The Port of Rotterdam, for example, is planning to shift much of its hinterland container traffic from road to rail and barge by 2030, changing the proportion of containers moved by these modes from, respectively, 49%, 37% and 14% in 2007 to 35%. 45% and 20% in 2030 (Braathens 2011). This is one respect in which the environmental leverage of a port can extend well beyond the direct emissions from port handling activities. By offering a competitive range of rail and waterborne services, which emit much less noxious pollutants and CO_2 per TEU- or tonne-km than road, a port can significantly reduce the environmental impact of the wider container supply chain.

Ports currently have little incentive to do so, however, because for environmental reporting purposes the boundary is usually drawn quite tightly around the port's activities. The Port of Long Beach is one of the few to report its carbon footprint within boundaries of differing extent. The first is the perimeter of the port, enclosing activities performed directly on-site. The second extends 24 nautical miles out to sea to include emissions from approaching and departing vessels within US territorial waters. The third also pushes the boundary inland to the State border (Port of Long Beach, 2009). Table 4.1 shows how the carbon emissions per TEU expands as the boundary is extended.

Table 4.1. **Effect of extending the reporting boundary on calculated CO_2 emissions from Long Beach Port**

CO_2 Reporting Boundary	kg CO_2 per TEU
Container handling only	16
Ocean going vessels included from 24 nm offshore	36
All port activity, off-shore shipping and transport to state border	119

Source: Port of Long Beach.

For this to be more than an analytical exercise, the boundary should reflect the amount of influence a port authority can exert over the level of emissions beyond its immediate territory. In most cases this influence is very limited, though as part of a multi-stakeholder initiative a port authority or terminal operator can play an important role in 'greening' the maritime supply chain. In the absence of this broader perspective, conflicts can arise between the environmental interests of the various parties. For example, transhipping a container from a ship to a train in a port terminal can emit significantly more CO_2 per TEU than transferring it to a truck, depending on the nature of the terminal layout and handling equipment. A terminal operator wishing to minimize its carbon footprint might therefore prefer to promote dispatch by road, whereas on a door-to-door basis emissions would be much lower if rail were used (Woolford and McKinnon 2011b).

Although ports are directly responsible for a very small percentage of the CO_2 emitted by the typical deep-sea container supply chain, many are refining their measurement of these emissions, setting ambitious targets for reducing them and implementing a range of decarbonisation measures (European Sea Ports Organisation 2012). For example, by electrifying its rubber-tyred gantry cranes, the Port of Hong Kong (2012) has been able to reduce average CO_2 emissions per container moved by roughly 60%. While such savings in carbon emissions are welcome they can be far exceeded by improvements in the environmental performance of hinterland transport.

Reducing Emissions from Hinterland Transport

These emissions can essentially be reduced in five ways:

- Rationalising the pattern of container movement.
- Shifting container traffic to lower carbon transport modes.
- Improving the loading of vehicles, wagons and barges carrying containers.
- Increasing the energy efficiency of the transport operations.
- Powering these operations with cleaner, lower-carbon fuels.

1. *Rationalising the pattern of container movement*: As discussed in Section 2, the amount of vehicle movement per container load within the hinterland can be reduced in various ways. This can be done by reducing the number of links in the container supply chain by, for example, adopting a port-centric logistics strategy (McKinnon 2013) and repositioning empty containers directly from import to export locations rather than via the port (Ng 2012). Even where the number of links remains constant, containers can be more efficiently routed between the various handling and storage nodes in the chain. The resulting reduction in the transport intensity of container distribution translates directly into lower emission levels.

2. *Shifting container traffic to lower carbon transport modes*: In most cases this entails a switch from road to rail, though in some countries, such as Belgium and the Netherlands, inland waterways and coastal shipping provide an important hinterland feeder service. Typically rail and waterborne transport emit between 25% and 50% of the CO_2 emissions per TEU of a trucking operation. The magnitude of their environmental advantage depends on a series of factors which vary internationally, including:

- The degree of rail-freight electrification and carbon intensity of the electricity used.
- Restrictions on the weights and dimensions of the relevant trucks, trains and barges.
- The relative vehicle age and emission profiles of the various modes.
- The relative density of the different modal networks.
- The number and locations of intermodal terminals, including dry ports.

The last of these factors is particularly important as rail and waterway services very seldom provide a door-to-door service and must rely on road feeder movements. This generally makes the freight movement more circuitous and erodes some of the environmental benefit of using rail or water (McKinnon 2011). Nevertheless, the use of intermodal services can still yield substantial reductions in truck-kms, fuel use and emissions (Department for Transport 2011). The channelling of container flows by rail to an inland 'dry port', rather than by road, has also been shown to offer large CO_2 savings (Rosa 2007).

3. *Improving the loading of vehicles, wagons and barges carrying containers*: If one takes the internal loading of the container as given and measures capacity utilisation on a TEU basis, significant potential exists for raising load factors. A survey of container trains leaving UK deep-sea ports found that, on average, only around 62% of the available slots on existing services were filled (Woodburn 2011). In some European countries, 13.6 metre trailers carrying 20ft (6 metre) containers are quite a common sight. Relaxing restrictions on truck length, for example, from 16.5 to 25 metres allows hauliers to combine a 40ft and 20ft container on the same vehicle, significantly cutting emissions relative to moving them in two separate vehicles. This, however, conflicts with the modal shift objective, as it substantially improves the price competitiveness of trucking, and can cause a net increase in emissions where much of the rail-based container traffic migrates to road (Knight et al. 2008). Where rail infrastructure permits, as in the US and Canada, double-stacking of container trains not only cuts emissions per ton-mile for existing rail traffic, as measured by Forkenbrock (2001), but also helps rail to expand its share of the hinterland transport market.

4. *Increasing the energy efficiency of hinterland transport operations*: Extensive research has been done on the opportunities for improving the energy efficiency of freight transport, most of which would apply as much to containerised traffic as to other forms of goods movement (e.g. Vyas et al. 2013). Much of this research has focused on the trucking sector which is understandable as it is by far the dominant freight mode and is more energy-intensive than rail and waterborne modes. A common finding of these studies, particularly those on road freight, is that there is a broad suite of technological, operational and behavioural measures available to cut energy consumption, ranging from driver training through aerodynamic profiling to the redesign of the vehicle engine and transmission systems (e.g. Aecom 2008).

5. Powering these operations with cleaner, lower carbon fuels: Like the previous measure, switching to alternative fuels is a means of decarbonising all forms of freight transport and has no special relevance to the hinterland transport of containers. The potential reductions in noxious and greenhouse gas emissions from freight operations achievable through 'repowering' with alternative fuels are discussed by Leonardi et al. (2013).

Case study: Emission Reduction in the ports of Los Angeles and Long Beach

Emissions have been an issue in California for over a decade with several studies analysing the health impact of diesel exhausts in the area. With the growth of cargo volumes in the ports of Los Angeles/Long Beach, particular attention has been paid to implementing policies to reduce emissions not only from vessels but also from hinterland connections. The California Air Resources Board has taken a leading role in regulating emissions. In addition to the emission reduction plans implemented in the ports (the Environmental Ship Index Program), that provide incentives for NOx, SOx and CO_2 emission reductions, one of the most controversial polices has been the imposition of penalties for idling trucks outside the port.

Regulation AB 2650 was introduced in 2003 and imposed a US$ 250 fine for the terminal operator for every truck idling for more than 30 minutes. The objective was to provide an incentive for ports to extend their gate times to 70 hours per week, offer additional gate time in the evening or at weekends and develop an appointment system for the drop off or pick up of containers. Terminal operators had sufficient flexibility to implement an appointment system and thus respond to the regulation. No terminal chose to comply with the regulation by extending gate hours, and all implemented some form of appointment system (Giuliano and O Brien 2007). This implied also that trucking companies had to interface with the appointment systems at all the terminals they were visiting.

Enforcement was limited and uptake of the appointment system not particularly high. The regulation in fact did not require trucking companies to use the appointment system and so use appointments has ranged from none to just above 30% (although variability exists among terminals) (Giuliano and O'Brien 2007). The appointment system had no impact on waiting times, and therefore limited impact, if any at all on emissions (Giuliano and O'Brien 2007). This is mostly because they failed to involve stakeholders, most notably road haulers and terminals; the authorities did not realise that terminals would implement the cheapest measure that allowed for lower chances of non-compliance, i.e. the appointment system; they also failed to recognise that terminals had little or no incentive to reduce delays on the land side as their major focus was providing service to the shipping lines. Government also did not set up adequate enforcement measures (Giuliano and O'Brien 2007; 2008).

Concluding remarks

The development of container terminal capacity needs to be complemented by the expansion of the hinterland links in order to enhance supply chain value creation and reduce external costs associated with increasing container flows. The importance of adequate hinterland infrastructural capabilities and efficient transport services to and from container terminal facilities cannot be over-stressed, especially in view of the global trends towards larger container vessels, mounting inter-terminal competition and increasing requirements for supply chain effectiveness.

This review paper has focused on hinterland transportation and services, analysing the various components of inland container transport where improvements can accompany container port expansions. As in the end it is the efficiency of the entire container supply chain, from shipper to consignees, that matters for the success of a container port inadequate hinterland infrastructure and services can be a major bottleneck. The paper argues that substantial improvements are possible in the interfaces between the container terminal and the inland transport modes, and through a better use of road and rail transport involving for example dry ports and empty container management.

The increasing importance of sustainability considerations in container supply chains also requires terminals and infrastructure development authorities to take more account of emissions and other external effects, so that the externalities can be actively managed and the economic benefits of increased connectivity are balanced against societal and environmental costs.

The paper identified three main segments of the hinterland supply chains and their corresponding infrastructure that affect the ability of container terminals to create supply chain value: the container gate systems, hinterland transport by road or rail, and dry ports. Each of these hinterland chain components are characterised by specific policy, management and environmental challenges, but a tendency that is common to all is the increasing need for coordination to minimise the risk of bottlenecks developing. It is only through a concerted effort among container terminals, local and national authorities, private road hauliers and railroads operators, as well as dry port managers and freight forwarders that the benefits of new infrastructure both at the port and inland can be maximised.

References

Acciaro, M. and Serra, P. 2013, "Maritime Supply Chain Security: A Critical Review", in IFSPA 2013, Trade Supply Chain Activities and Transport: Contemporary Logistics and Maritime Issues, pp. 636.

Aecom 2008. Reducing Greenhouse Gas Emissions from Heavy-Duty Vehicles, Report for the European Commission, Brussels.

Almotairi, B. and Lumsden, K. 2009, "Port logistics platform integration in supply chain management", International Journal of Shipping and Transport Logistics, vol. 1, no. 2, pp. 194-210.

Bagchi, P.K. and Paik, S. 2001, "The role of public-private partnership in port information systems development", International Journal of Public Sector Management, vol. 14, no. 6, pp. 482-499.

Bakshi, N., Flynn, S.E. and Gans, N. 2011, "Estimating the operational impact of container inspections at international ports", Management Science, vol. 57, no. 1, pp. 1-20.

Benacchio, M., Ferrari, C., Haralambides, H.E. and Musso, E. 2001, "On the economic impact of ports: local vs. national costs and benefits", Forum of Shipping and Logistics, Special Interest Group on Maritime Transport and Ports International Workshop, pp. 8.

Berechman, J. and Tseng, P-H. 2012, "Estimating the environmental costs of port related emissions: The case of Kaohsiung" Transportation Research D, 17, 35-38.

Beresford, A., Pettit, S., Xu, Q. and Williams, S. 2012, "A study of dry port development in China", Maritime Economics and Logistics, vol. 14, no. 1, pp. 73-98.

Bergqvist, R. 2008, "Realizing logistics opportunities in a public–private collaborative setting: The story of Skaraborg", Transport Reviews, vol. 28, no. 2, pp. 219-237.

Bergqvist, R. 2012, "Hinterland logistics and global supply chains" in Maritime Logistics: A Complete Guide to Effective Shipping and Port Management, eds. D. Song and P. Panayides, Kogan Page Publishers, , pp. 211-232.

Bergqvist, R. 2013, "Hinterland Transport in Sweden: The Context of Intermodal Terminals and Dry Ports" in Dry Ports - A Global Perspective, Challenges and Developments in Serving Hinterlands., eds. R. Bergqvist, G. Wilmsmeier and K. Cullinane, Ashgate Publishing Ltd., Farnham, pp. 13-28.

Bergqvist, R., Wilmsmeier, G. and Cullinane, K. (eds) 2013a, Dry Ports - A Global Perspective, Challenges and Developments in Serving Hinterlands., Ashgate Publishing Ltd., Farnham.

Bergqvist, R., Wilmsmeier, G. and Cullinane, K. 2013b, "Introduction—A Global Perspective on Dryports" in Dry Ports - A Global Perspective, Challenges and Developments in Serving Hinterlands., eds. R. Bergqvist, G. Wilmsmeier and K. Cullinane, Ashgate Publishing Ltd., Farnham, pp. 1-10.

Bichou, K. 2011, "Assessing the impact of procedural security on container port efficiency", Maritime Economics and Logistics, vol. 13, no. 1, pp. 1-28.

Braathens, N.A. 2011, "Environmental Impact of Shipping: Role of Ports' OECD, Paris.

Brooks, M.R. and Schellinck, T. 2013, "Measuring port effectiveness in user service delivery: What really determines users' evaluations of port service delivery?", Research in Transportation Business and Management.

Buhaug, Ø. et al. 2009, 'Prevention of Air Pollution from Ships: second IMO GHG Study' International Maritime Organisation, London.

California Air Resources Board 2006, "Quantification of the Health Impacts and Economic Valuation of Air Pollution from Ports and Goods Movement in California" Appendix A in "Emission Reduction Plan Ports and Goods Movement in California." California Air Resources Board.

Carbone, V. and de Martino, M. 2003, "The changing role of ports in supply-chain management: an empirical analysis", Maritime Policy and Management, vol. 30, no. 4, pp. 305-320.

CE Delft 2012, "Potential of Modal Shift to Rail Transport: Study on the projected effects on GHG emissions and transport volumes", Delft.

Chen, G. and Yang, Z. 2010, "Optimizing time windows for managing export container arrivals at Chinese container terminals", Maritime Economics and Logistics, vol. 12, no. 1, pp. 111-126.

Chen, G., Govindan, K. and Yang, Z. 2013, "Managing truck arrivals with time windows to alleviate gate congestion at container terminals", International Journal of Production Economics, vol. 141, no. 1, pp. 179-188.

Clark, X., Dollar, D. and Micco, A. 2004, "Port Efficiency, Maritime Transport Costs, and Bilateral Trade", Journal of Development Economics, vol. 75 2, pp. 417-50.

Cullinane, K. and Khanna, M. 1999, "Economies of Scale in Large Container Ships", Journal of Transport Economics and Policy, vol. 33 2, pp. 185-207.

Davies, P. 2013, Container terminal Reservation Systems Design and Performance, Paper Presented at the METRANS International Urban Freight Conference, Long Beach, October 8, 2013.

Department for Transport 2009a, Mode Shift Benefit Values: Technical report, London.

Department for Transport 2009b, 'Guide to the Mode Shift Revenue Support (MSRS) Scheme' London.

Department for Transport 2011, "Choosing and Developing a Multi-modal Transport Solution" Freight Best Practice Programme, London.

Estache, A., Goldstein, A. and Pittman, R. 2001, "Privatization and Regulatory Reform in Brazil: the case of freight railways", Journal of Industry, Competition and Trade, vol. 1, no. 2, pp. 203-235.

European Sea Ports Organisation 2012, "Green Guide." Brussels.

Forkenbrock, D.J. 2001, "Comparison of external costs of rail and truck freight transportation", Transportation Research Part A, vol. 35, no. 4, pp. 321–337.

Frankel, E.G. 1999, "The Economics of Total Trans-ocean Supply Chain Management", International Journal of Maritime Economics, vol. 1, no. 2, pp. 61-69.

Fransoo, J.C. and Lee, C. 2012, "The Critical Role of Ocean Container Transport in Global Supply Chain Performance", Production and Operations Management, vol. 22, no. 2, pp. 253-368.

Free and Hanseatic City of Hamburg and Hamburg Port Authority 2012, Hamburg is Staying on Course, the Port Development Plan to 2025, Free and Hanseatic City of Hamburg - State Ministry of Economic Affairs, Transport and Innovation; Hamburg Port Authority, Hamburg.

Freightliner (2013) 'Written Evidence to Parliamentary Inquiry' http://www.publications.parliament.uk/pa/cm201314/cmselect/cmtran/writev/ports/ports.pdf

Gilman, S. 1999, "The size economies and network efficiency of large containerships", Maritime Economics and Logistics, vol. 1, no. 1, pp. 39-59.

Giuliano, G. and O'Brien, T. 2007, "Reducing port-related truck emissions: The terminal gate appointment system at the Ports of Los Angeles and Long Beach", Transportation Research Part D: Transport and Environment, vol. 12, no. 7, pp. 460-473.

Giuliano, G. and O'Brien, T. 2008, "Extended gate operations at the ports of Los Angeles and Long Beach: a preliminary assessment", Maritime Policy and Management, vol. 35, no. 2, pp. 215-235.

Goel, A. and Kok, L. 2012a, "Efficient scheduling of team truck drivers in the European Union", Flexible services and manufacturing journal, vol. 24, no. 1, pp. 81-96.

Goel, A. and Kok, L. 2012b, "Truck driver scheduling in the United States", Transportation Science, vol. 46, no. 3, pp. 317-326.

Guan, C. and Liu, R.R. 2009, "Container terminal gate appointment system optimization", Maritime Economics and Logistics, vol. 11, no. 4, pp. 378-398.

Hall, P.V. and Jacobs, W. 2010, "Shifting Proximities: The Maritime Ports Sector in an Era of Global Supply Chains", Regional Studies, vol. 44, no. 9, pp. 1103-1115.

Van Ham, H., and Koppenjan, J. 2001, "Building Public-Private Partnerships: Assessing and managing risks in port development", Public Management Review, vol. 3 no. 4, pp. 593-616.

Haralambides, H. and Gujar, G. 2011, "The Indian dry ports sector, pricing policies and opportunities for public-private partnerships", Research in Transportation Economics, vol. 33, no. 1, pp. 51-58.

Haralambides, H.E. and Londoño-Kent, M.P. 2004, "Supply Chain Bottlenecks: Border Crossing Inefficiencies between Mexico and the United States", International Journal of Transport Economics, vol. 31 2, pp. 183-95.

Haralambides, H.E. 2002, "Competition, Excess Capacity, and the Pricing of Port Infrastructure", International Journal of Maritime Economics, vol. 4 4, pp. 323-47.

Heaver, T., Meersman, H. and van de Voorde, E. 2001, "Co-operation and competition in international container transport: strategies for ports", Maritime Policy and Management, vol. 28, no. 3, pp. 293-305.

Heaver, T.D. 2002, "The Evolving Roles of Shipping Lines in International Logistics", International Journal of Maritime Economics, vol. 4, no.3, pp. 210-30.

Helling, A. and Poister, T.H. 2000, "US maritime ports: trends, policy implications, and research needs", Economic Development Quarterly, vol. 14, no. 3, pp. 300-317.

Hu, L., Shi, X., Voß, S. and Zhang, W. 2011, "Application of RFID technology at the entrance gate of container terminals" in Computational Logistics Springer, vol. 6971, pp. 209-220.

Huynh, N. 2009, "Reducing truck turn times at marine terminals with appointment scheduling", Transportation Research Record: Journal of the Transportation Research Board, vol. 2100, no. 1, pp. 47-57.

International Council on Clean Transportation 2007, 'Air Pollution and Greenhouse Gas Emissions from Ocean-going Ships' ICCT, Washington DC.

ITF 2008, 'Port Competition and Hinterland Connections: Summary and Conclusions' Discussion Paper no. 2008-19. Joint Transport Research Centre, OECD / International Transport Forum, Paris.

Kia, M., Shayan, E. and Ghotb, F. 2000, "The importance of information technology in port terminal operations", International Journal of Physical Distribution and Logistics Management, vol. 30, no. 3/4, pp. 331-344.

Knight, I., Newton, W., McKinnon, A.C., Palmer, A. et al. 2008. "Longer and / or Longer and Heavier Goods Vehicles (LHVs): A study of the likely effects if permitted in the UK: Final Report" TRL, Crowthorne.

Konings, R. 2007, "Opportunities to improve container barge handling in the port of Rotterdam from a transport network perspective", Journal of Transport Geography, vol. 15, no. 6, pp. 443-454.

Koppenjan, J. F. M., and Leijten, M. 2007. "How to sell a Railway: Lessons on the privatization of Three Dutch Railway Projects", European Journal of Transport and Infrastructure Research (Online), vol. 7 no. 3, pp. 201-222.

Korovyakovsky, E. and Panova, Y. 2011, "Dynamics of Russian dry ports", Research in Transportation Economics, vol. 33, no. 1, pp. 25-34.

Lee, E., Nam, H. and Song, D. 2012, "Defining Maritime Logistics and its Value" in Marimte Logistics a Complete Guide to effective Shipping and Port Management, eds. D. Song and P.M. Panayides, Kogan Page Publishers, , pp. 9-22.

Leonardi, J., Cullinane, S. and Edwards, J.B. 2013, "The Benefits and Costs of Switching to Alternative Fuels" in McKinnon, A.C., Browne, M. and Whitening, A. Green Logistics, Kogan Page, London.

Lewis, B.M., Erera, A.L. and White, C.C. 2003, "Optimization approaches for efficient container security operations at transhipment seaports", Transportation Research Record: Journal of the Transportation Research Board, vol. 1822, no. -1, pp. 1-8.

Lirn, T.C. and Wang, J.H. 2010, "The study of threat factors on port risk management: an empirical research in the Kaohsiung Port", Proceedings for International Forum on Maritime Security, pp. 93.

Maloni, M., Paul, J.A. and Gligor, D.M. 2013, "Slow steaming impacts on ocean carriers and shippers", Maritime Economics and Logistics, 15, 151-171.

Mangan, J., Lalwani, C. and Fynes, B. 2008, "Port-centric logistics", International Journal of Logistics Management, vol. 19, no. 1, pp. 29-41.

Marchet, G., Perotti, S. and Mangiaracina, R. 2012, "Modelling the impacts of ICT adoption for inter-modal transportation", International Journal of Physical Distribution and Logistics Management, vol. 42, no. 2, pp. 110-127.

McKinnon, A. C. (2006) ' A Review of Truck Tolling Schemes and Assessment of their Possible Impact on Logistics Systems' International Journal of Logistics: Research and Applications, vol 9, no. 3, pp.191-205.

McKinnon, A.C. 2009, "The Present and Future Land Requirements of Logistical Activities", Land Use Policy, vol. 26S, pp. s293-s301.

McKinnon, A.C. 2010, "European Freight Transport Statistics: Limitations, Misinterpretations and Aspirations" ACEA, Brussels.

McKinnon, A.C. 2013, "Decarbonising the deep-sea container supply chain: the possible contribution of port-centric logistics" in: Proceedings of the 13th Annual Conference on Transportation Research Society, Rio de Janeiro.

Meersman, H., Pauwels, T., van de Voorde, E. and Vanelslander, T. 2008, "The relation between port competition and hinterland connections: the case of the' Iron Rhine' and the' Betuweroute'", International Forum on Shipping, Ports and Airports (IFSPA 2008)-Trade-Based Global Supply Chain and Transport Logistics Hubs: Trends and Future Development.

Monios, J. and Lambert, B. 2013, "Intermodal Freight Corridor Development in the United States." in Dry Ports - A Global Perspective, Challenges and Developments in Serving Hinterlands., eds. R. Bergqvist, G. Wilmsmeier and K. Cullinane, Ashgate Publishing Ltd., Farnham, pp. 197-218.

Monios, J. and Wilmsmeier, G. 2012, "Port-centric logistics, dry ports and offshore logistics hubs: strategies to overcome double peripherality?" Maritime Policy and Management, vol. 39, no. 2, pp. 207-226.

Morais, P. and Lord, E. 2006, Terminal appointment system study.

Ng, A.S.F. 2012, Container flows and empty container repositioning. In: Song, D.W. and Panagotis, P. (eds), Maritime Transport: Contemporary Issues. Edward Elgar Publishing Group Ltd, London.

Ng, A.Y. and Gujar, G.C. 2009, "Government policies, efficiency and competitiveness: The case of dry ports in India", Transport Policy, vol. 16, no. 5, pp. 232-239.

Notteboom, T. 2008, "The Relationship between Seaports and the Inter-modal Hinterland in light of Global Supply Chain: European Challenges" Discussion paper no. 2008-10. Joint Transport Research Centre, OECD / International Transport Forum, Paris.

Notteboom, T. 2007, "Container river services and gateway ports: Similarities between the Yangtze River and the Rhine River", Asia Pacific Viewpoint, vol. 48, no. 3, pp. 330-343.

Notteboom, T. and Rodrigue, J-P. 2008, "Containerisation, Box Logistics and Global Supply Chains: The Integration of Ports and Liner Shipping Networks", Maritime Economics and Logistics, vol. 10, no. 1-2, pp. 152-174.

Notteboom, T. and Rodrigue, J-P., 2007, "Re-assessing port hinterland relationships in the context of global supply chains". In: Wang, J., Notteboom, T., Olivier, D. and Slack, B., (eds), Ports, cities and global supply chains. pp. 51-68. Aldershot: Ashgate.

Notteboom, T.A. 2006, "The Time Factor in Liner Shipping Services", Maritime Economics and Logistics, vol. 8, no. 1, pp. 19-39.

Padilha, F. and Ng, A.K. 2012, "The spatial evolution of dry ports in developing economies: The Brazilian experience", Maritime Economics and Logistics, vol. 14, no. 1, pp. 99-121.

Pittman, R. 2004, "Russian railways reform and the problem of non-discriminatory access to infrastructure", Annals of Public and Cooperative Economics, vol. 75, no. 2, pp. 167-192.

Pittman, R. 2007, "Options for restructuring the state-owned monopoly railway", Research in Transportation Economics, vol. 20, pp. 179-198.

Pittman, R. 2013, "The freight railways of the former Soviet Union, twenty years on: Reforms lose steam", Research in Transportation Business and Management, vol. 6, no. 0, pp. 99-115.

Port of Hong Kong 2012, "Port of Hong Kong: Handbook and Directory".

Port of Long Beach 2009, "Air Emissions Inventory" Long Beach.

Robinson, R. 2002, "Ports as elements in value-driven chain systems: the new paradigm", Maritime Policy and Management, vol. 29, no. 3, pp. 241-255.

Rodrigue, J. and Notteboom, T. 2010, "Comparative North American and European gateway logistics: the regionalism of freight distribution", Journal of Transport Geography, vol. 18, no. 4, pp. 497-507.

Rodrigue, J. 1999, "Globalization and the synchronization of transport terminals", Journal of Transport Geography, vol. 7, no. 4, pp. 255-261.

Rodrigue, J., Debrie, J., Fremont, A. and Gouvernal, E. 2010, "Functions and actors of inland ports: European and North American dynamics", Journal of Transport Geography, vol. 18, no. 4, pp. 519-529.

Rosa, V. 2007, "Evaluation of the dry port concept from an environmental perspective: A note" Transportation Research Part D: Transport and the Environment, vol. 12, no. 7, pp. 523-527.

Roso, V. and Lumsden, K. 2010, "A review of dry ports", Maritime Economics and Logistics, vol. 12, no. 2, pp. 196-213.

Roso, V. and Rosa, A. 2012, "Dry port in concept and practice" in Maritime Logistics: A Complete Guide to Effective Shipping and Port Management, eds. D. Song and P. Panayides, Kogan Page Publishers, pp. 179-193.

Roso, V. 2008, "Factors influencing implementation of a dry port", International Journal of Physical Distribution and Logistics Management, vol. 38, no. 10, pp. 782-798.

Roso, V., Woxenius, J. and Lumsden, K. 2009, "The dry port concept: connecting container seaports with the hinterland", Journal of Transport Geography, vol. 17, no. 5, pp. 338-345.

Schilk, G., Blumel, E., Recagno, V. and Boevé, W. 2007, "Ship, port and supply chain security concepts interlinking maritime with hinterland transport chains", International Symposium on Maritime Safety, Security and Environmental Protection. Athens (Greece), 20th September.

Shi, X., Tao, D. and Voß, S. 2011, "RFID technology and its application to port-based container logistics", Journal of Organizational Computing and Electronic Commerce, vol. 21, no. 4, pp. 332-347.

Song, D. and Panayides, P.M. 2008, "Global supply chain and port/terminal: integration and competitiveness", Maritime Policy and Management, vol. 35, no. 1, pp. 73-87.

Song, D. 2003, "Port Co-opetition in Concept and Practice", Maritime Policy and Management, vol. 30, no. 1, pp. 29-44.

Stahlbock, R. and Voß, S. 2008, "Operations research at container terminals: a literature update", Or Spectrum, vol. 30, no. 1, pp. 1-52.

Suykens, F. and van de Voorde, E. 1998, "A quarter a century of port management in Europe: objectives and tools", Maritime Policy and Management, vol. 25, no. 3, pp. 251-261.

Tongzon, J., Chang, Y. and Lee, S. 2009, "How supply chain oriented is the port sector?", International Journal of Production Economics, vol. 122, no. 1, pp. 21-34.

Transport Scotland (2012) Freight Facilities Grants Awarded to Projects in Scotland since August 1997. Glasgow.

UNECE 1998, UN/LOCODE - Code for ports and other locations, Regulation 16, UN, Geneva.

van Asperen, E., Borgman, B. and Dekker, R. 2011, "Evaluating impact of truck announcements on container stacking efficiency", Flexible Services and Manufacturing Journal, vol. 25, no. 4, pp. 543-556.

van der Horst, M. R. and de Langen, P. W. 2008, 'Coordination in hinterland transport-chains: A major challenge for the seaport community'. Maritime Economics and Logistics, 10, no. 1 108–129.

Veenstra, A., Zuidwijk, R. and van Asperen, E. 2012, "The extended gate concept for container terminals: Expanding the notion of dry ports", Maritime Economics and Logistics, vol. 14, no. 1, pp. 14-32.

Vyas, A D, Patel, D M and Bertram, K M 2013, "Potential for Energy Efficiency Improvement Beyond the Light-Duty-Vehicle Sector" Argonne National Laboratory, Argonne Il.

Wiegmans, B.W., Rietveld, P., Pels, E. and van Woudenberg, S. 2004, "Container Terminals and Utilisation of Facilities", International Journal of Transport Economics, vol. 31 3, pp. 313-39.

Wiegmans, B.W., van der Hoest, A. and Notteboom, T. E. 2008, "Port and terminal selection by deep-sea container operators" Maritime Policy and Management, vol. 35, no. 6, pp. 517-534.

Woodburn, A. 2011, "An Investigation of Container Train Service Provision and Load Factors in Great Britain", European Journal of Transport Infrastructure Research, vol. 11, no. 2, pp. 147-165.

Woolford, R. and McKinnon, A.C. 2011b, "Container port emissions: What is included and just how big are they?" in Cherrett, T. (ed) Proceedings of the Logistics Research Network Annual Conference, University of Southampton.

Woolford, R.E. and McKinnon, A.C. 2011a, "Decarbonising the Maritime Supply Chain: the Role of the Shipper", in Notteboom, T. (ed) Current Issues in Shipping, Ports and Logistics, Associated Scientific Publishers, Brussels.

Yang, Y. 2010, "Impact of the container security initiative on Taiwan's shipping industry", Maritime Policy and Management, vol. 37, no. 7, pp. 699-722.

Yap, W.Y. and Lam, J.S.L. 2013, "80 million-twenty-foot-equivalent-unit container port? Sustainability issues in port and coastal development", Ocean and Coastal Management, vol. 71, no. 0, pp. 13-25.

Yeo, G., Pak, J. and Yang, Z. 2013, "Analysis of dynamic effects on seaports adopting port security policy", Transportation Research Part A: Policy and Practice, vol. 49, pp. 285-301.

Zhao, W. and Goodchild, A.V. 2010, "The impact of truck arrival information on container terminal rehandling", Transportation Research Part E: Logistics and Transportation Review, vol. 46, no. 3, pp. 327-343.

Chapter 5

Structure, financing and risk management in large port infrastructure concessions: The Chilean case

José Luis Guasch[1]
Ancor Suárez Alemán[2]
Lourdes Trujillo[3]

The success of private sector participation in infrastructure is highly conditioned by the ability of governments to properly shape and control the public-private contractual relationship. Therefore, determining the accurate mechanism to control private participation becomes imperative, both ex-ante (by designing correct contracts, properly assigning risks; designing effective competitive tendering and robust and transparent award criteria, and implementing effective oversight and regulation) and ex-post (post contract award management and careful handling of renegotiation requests). In addition, risk management in private concession processes is a major issue, particularly with very large infrastructure projects where the risks may be an obstacle to private finance.

This paper discusses the options for private participation in a new mega-port initiative in Chile (a port capable of handling 12 000 or 18 000 TEU ships) and arguments a generic finding, that in port infrastructure it is sensible to separate the delivery of the breakwater component from the rest of the port infrastructure development (terminals). Due to a lack benefits from bundling, easier access to finance (as a consequence of construction risk), and the potential inability of the private sector to better manage the perceived construction risk in this case, the recommended approach is traditional delivery for the breakwaters and port concessions (PPPs) for the terminals.

1. Corresponding author Professor of Economics, University of California San Diego

2. Department of Applied Economics, University of Las Palmas de Gran Canaria, Spain

3. Department of Applied Economics, University of Las Palmas de Gran Canaria, Spain

Introduction

The complex industry of transport has traditionally provoked a large number of debates to determine the role that governments and firms play in it. Economic theory has already recognized the advantages of private sector involvement in some industries, but it is also accepted that some sectors require regulation to prevent results which do not increase social welfare. Therefore, the establishment of a proper regulatory framework and mechanisms, which would create adequate incentives for companies operating in the transport market is essential.

The inclusion of private participation in the infrastructure sector seems to improve efficiency, productivity and service quality (Andrés et al, 2007; Trujillo and Gonzalez, 2007). However, from a welfare maximisation perspective, privatisation processes are not given the necessary attention they require. Societies perceive privatisation as if the new owner would achieve full discretion in decisions about the acquired public goods. In fact, that could even be true, if there were no contracts and contractual obligations between the public and the private partner. In this context, the welfare maximisation perspective is crucially dependent on the establishment of a proper regulatory framework for concessions.

Frequently, the negative public opinion on privatisations stems from failures in their implementation. The lack of transparency or an inadequate communication with the public might be some other reasons explaining the current unfavourable stance of the public. Accordingly, as noted before, privatisation in some sectors requires proper economic regulation. The success of privatisations is highly dependent on the ability of governments to control private concessions. Finally, the possibility to renegotiate the initial terms or conditions in case it appears necessary is another important factor at play, which influences the public perception of privatisations (Guasch, 2006).

In some cases where the concessionaries earned huge profits, customers and workers were left at a disadvantage. In others efficiency gains did not materialize. There were also cases, where the workers suffered from adverse employment regulations and wage cuts. Therefore, setting up a proper regulatory framework for privatisations is of critical importance, both *ex-ante* (by designing correct contracts; negotiation or auctions) and *ex-post* (renegotiations).

Commonly, privatisations are seen as a trade-off between efficiency and social objectives: those in favour stress that it increases operational efficiency and innovation, and those opposed emphasize its capacity to abuse consumers and/or employees and its tendency to hurt the environment (Cullinane and Song, 2002).

Chile has a successful track record of introducing private finance in infrastructure investments (including ports) through concession contracts. However, under the current concession schemes, there is a high degree of risk associated with very large civil engineering works involved in building breakwaters for this mega-port initiative. This report presents the experience on private participation in ports, including in Chile, and addresses a number of issues relevant to the implementation of mega-ports (*Puerto de Gran Escala)* in Chile. These include questions such as: Should the concession model be modified and should we consider underwriting this risk or finance the breakwaters by the public sector? What type of concession should be granted? How should the tendering of terminals be structured to secure the desired level of competition?

Port reform process

In recent years a significant number of countries have implemented policies directed at reforming their port industry, with the idea to improve efficiency and to reduce the heavy financial burden placed upon governments. During the 1960s and 1970s, the port infrastructure was badly maintained and often poorly managed in most developing countries and in some developed ones. Against this background, from the early 1980s onward, technology advances like cargo containerization pushed the maritime transport industry into a fundamental restructuring of its service networks. Suddenly, there was no longer any distinction possible between ports in developing countries and in industrialized nations. Ports worldwide were confronted by the same process of change (Juhel, 2001).

A traditional seaport, before the introduction of reforms reflecting changes in the maritime transport industry, could be described by the following characteristics:

- National or local government budgets are used to finance the building of most large infrastructure construction costs, but public budgets are becoming tighter.
- Port authority (generally public) finances the costs of maintenance and repairs for infrastructure and it is financed partly with public funds, and the rest by port tariffs and fees from private firms operating in the port.
- There is an excess of employees working in the port, who have a high degree of unionization and strong positions at collective bargaining.
- Port efficiency in terms of costs and waiting times for ships is relatively poor (Trujillo and Gonzalez, 2011).

As a consequence, there is currently a great need for large capital investments in the seaport industry to accommodate the growing demand. In addition past maintenance and renewal levels have often been inadequate, thus creating a maintenance backlog which is an additional cause for the need of required investment.

This is especially true in the context of reduced public subsidies, which are due to tighter fiscal conditions among governments. In this context, private finance becomes an important option.

The current trend observed worldwide is the general adoption of the landlord model as an organisational scheme for ports. Such arrangements have a long tradition in North America and Western Europe. Since 1980, more than a hundred ports in developing and transitional countries has also reorganized in this way. In this model, the port authorities retain the ownership of the infrastructure in order to avoid the risk of monopolisation of essential assets by private firms. The private firms are in charge of operations in the port. Concession contracts between port authorities and private firms are the most common instrument to implement this type of private participation in ports.

The role of port authorities is thus transformed from institutions traditionally in charge of all port activities to one in which they are only a coordinator of these activities. Introducing private firms in seaports thus requires the design of new regulatory systems to monitor their behaviour. The regulation takes place in asymmetric information conditions as firms know their costs and market conditions better than the regulator does. However, it is not strictly required that port authorities perform this regulatory task, and another independent institution could also be used instead.

The previous description of stylised facts does not aim at reflecting the exact situation of all seaports in the world, but to identify the main questions that those seaports that have started introducing reforms have already faced (such as containerisation of cargo and development of larger and more specialised ships, as already noted above). Moreover, technological changes, introduced in the last decades, such as containerisation of cargo and development of larger and more specialized specialised ships, have forced seaports to start a fast renewal cycle of their facilities. Specifically, the ports wanted to be able to provide services, which are compatible with the new needs of shipping companies and they wanted to respond to a growing demand for container handling services.

Introducing private participation in ports

There are several alternatives, when introducing private participation in the organisation of port services, depending on port size, initial conditions, and the type of service considered[1]. Two main directions emerge from the different possibilities: selling the seaport as a whole (*full privatisation*) or introducing private participation to build/renovate facilities or to provide specific services (*concession/PPP*). With full privatisation, all the assets and liabilities are transferred to the private sector. It is also possible to transfer parts of the seaport to be developed by private operators (e.g. Build, Operate and Own - BOO).

The second option implies introducing private participation for a given number of years. The different possibilities are:

a) Services that require an exclusive use of infrastructure or superstructure port facilities

- Introduction of private participation in the port in order to build or renovate facilities required for service provision (Build/Rehabilitate, Operate and Transfer, BOT or ROT):

  In this case, the public sector does not lose ownership of the port infrastructure, and new facilities built by private firms are transferred to the public sector after a specified period of time. This is the case of classical concessions, which is discussed further for the Chilean Puerto de Gran Escala.

- Creation of a new independent company, combining the efforts of two or more firms: *joint-ventures:*

  This type of agreement arises when at least two parties with common interests join forces. Thus, for example, in some cases a firm can supply technology and know-how, while another might have knowledge of market opportunities and customer contacts.

These agreements are not signed exclusively between private firms. There are examples of collaboration between port authorities and private firms, as in the cases of Shanghai (China), Kelang (Malaysia), Sri-Lanka, and other Asian ports with large investment projects, where port authorities have formed many joint-ventures to develop and operate new terminals. In other cases, joint-ventures may be found between several public firms, as in the example of the Singapore Port Authority with the authority of Dalian, to develop and operate a container terminal in the port of Dayaowan (China).

b) Services that do not require an exclusive use of infrastructure or superstructure port facilities

- *Leasing*

  In some cases, port authorities simply rent port assets to be used by private operators during a fixed period, and thus obtain income from contract fees. Contrary to concession contracts, the private firms in this case are usually not required to make investments; therefore they only assume commercial risks. Operators under this scheme rent some port facilities, such as storage buildings or cranes.

- *Licensing*

  Here the port authority allows the operators to provide some services which only require relatively simple equipment, and thus assets are generally owned by private operators. Infrastructure is provided to these operators to use it, generally for some specified fee, and in some cases they may also use some superstructure elements owned by the port authority. Stevedoring companies, pilots, tug operators or consignees can work under this type of agreements.

- *Management contract*

  A simple form of introducing private participation in a port is by contracting out the port management. In this situation, the port authority is the owner of infrastructure and port facilities, but decisions with regard to its management are taken by a private firm which can apply a more commercial approach to operations. Both the investment and commercial risks are faced by the public sector, since managers do not invest their own capital in the port. The port of Bristol (UK) is an example of this type of contract, where the local government owns facilities, but the port is managed privately.

When choosing among the options listed above to determine the best alternative for a particular port, the port objectives must be evaluated, and the constraints that the port authority faces must be considered. The type of service, financing environment, size of projects may determine the possible degree and the specific modalities of private participation

Some experiences in private participation in ports

Traditionally, the UK has taken the leading role in terms of privatisation processes (particularly in the port sector). The total revenue produced from all UK privatisations in the last two decades amounted to more than USD 121 billion and, considering all Europe, the total increased up to USD 641 billion (Baird and Valentine, 2007). Authors noted that port privatisation in the UK was never about developing new and improved port infrastructure and facilities to benefit the economy, which was the aim in other countries; it was simply a mechanism used to remove port assets from public ownership.

Along the same line, Cullinane and Song (2002) emphasised that privatisation provided only a partial cure for the ails of the port industry. Authors also pointed out that the entire port system has to be flexible enough to allow modifications in response to a changing business environment. Brooks (2004), based on the work of Saundry and Turnbul (1997), commented that although "privatisation did not transform the financial and economic performance of UK trust ports sufficiently to justify the private gains of port management shareholders, and represented a ''huge public loss'', it is not clear if the outcome would have been better if the UK government had provided greater regulatory oversight post-privatisation".

Latin America has also been considered a suitable case to analyse privatisation processes. As Guasch et al (2008) noted, the Latin American and Caribbean countries have taken the lead in allowing private sector participation in the provision of infrastructure services. From the first steps in Chile in the 1980s, the region has experienced a wave of privatisations in sectors such as petrol, gas, agriculture and public services, among others (Estache and Trujillo, 2004). This process of privatisations was in full swing especially in the 1990s, with the adoption of the price cap regulatory model. Estache et al (2004) noted that "the infrastructure reforms of the 1990s consisted essentially of vertical and horizontal unbundling of the sectors into multiple business units—when allowed by country size-- and 'privatisation' of as many as possible of these business units".

The proceeds from the large scale privatisations in the 1990s reached 6% of the GPD in 18 Latin-American countries (IDB, 2002). However, in most cases, efficiency gains have been secured and users have seen improvement in the quality and access to the service. The effect on prices has been mixed to some extent due to the initial (prior to private sector participation) price distortions. In a number of cases, private sector participation has been associated with political ideology. Yet that has changed since the late 1900s, when pragmatism (due to the need to improve public services) trumped ideology (Estache and Trujillo, 2004).

Stressing the Latin America case, Estache et al (2003) also noted that privatisation without competition generated few benefits for the economies, showing that price caps alone would not do much for users. The literature on Latin America privatisations processes is vast and extended (Delfino and Casarin, 2003; Barja and Urquiola, 2004; Paredes, 2003; Torero and Pasco-Font, 2003; Ennis and Pinto, 2003; Resende and Facanha, 2002; Mueller, 2001, Engel et al, 2000, among many others).

As Hoffman (2001) showed, after the private participation process, there is less public involvement in port planning, investment and regulation in Latin America than in Europe. However, the public sector has a role to play concerning the monitoring of anti-competitive behaviour and the provision of a legal and regulatory framework, among other functions. The success of privatisations is highly dependent on how they are established according to terms and conditions and, specially, how they are implemented and regulated.

Although not specifically linked to ports and limited to Latin America, the findings and suggestions above are in line with economic theory and evidence with regard to public utilities, which share some of the characteristics of port infrastructure projects (e.g. large capital investments, sunk costs and related obstacles to competition). For example, Estache and Rossi (2010) using a representative sample of 220 electricity distribution companies from 51 development countries for the period 1985-2005 find, that private regulated companies are more efficient than state-owned regulated companies, Similar findings are derived in a major study of World Bank (Gassner et al., 2009) from a sample of 1,200 utilities from 71 developed and transition economies. Using the analogy of Parker (2004) for the case of Great Britain: "... without privatisation, the introduction of competition in some (network) activities would not have been possible at all, or would have been difficult to promote. For example, in the distribution of gas and electricity, and the regulation would remain highly politicised. In other words, increased competition and better regulation are likely to be direct consequences of the privatisation process. In short, the theory recommends competition as the first best choice, and when this is not possible, regulation,[2] and only after that privatisation (with regulation)."

Finally, some other questions arise about the structure and procedures.[3] There is no single procedure or a blue print regarding awarding procedures that could be universally considered as best practice (Farrel, 2012). There has been ample discussion on awarding port terminal concessions in the recent years (Notteboom et al, 2012). The international experience provides a number of different procedures according to country and environment circumstances. Considering the case of one of the fastest-growing economies worldwide, China, ports operate through joint ventures where the public sector holds 75% of the total share as minimum, while terminal operators work as commercial firms. Other regions, such as Europe, have opted for a bigger role of private partnership through PPP models (Kappeler and Nemoz, 2010). Therefore, some of the main issues are to determine the role of private and public sector, the risk allocation between port authority and operators, and the extent of financial or credit enhancement support.

The international trends on mega-ports: A quick review

The global trade context characterised by the improvement of logistics chains, the development of containerization and hub concepts and the arrival of the new supra-large ships is producing a flurry of mega-ports around the world. They are being considered, launched or are in progress; some are greenfield, while some involve significant expansions around existing ports. Capacity ranges from 2 to 15 million TEU. A number of them do have breakwaters investments components.

Latin America and the Caribbean area also a part of that trend, with mega-port projects in the works in Peru, Callao (San Lorenzo Island), Colombia (Cartagena), Panama (two, Balboa and Rodman in the Pacific side), Mexico (Punta Colonet, Baja California), Cuba and of course Chile. There are many other mega-port initiatives around the world. In the Gulf countries (Dubai, Kuwait, Qatar and Abu Dabhi-Khakifa Port), Indonesia (Jakarta), Taiwan, Sri-Lanka, Lagos (Nigeria), Kenya, Tanzania, Australia (Gladstone) among others and of course the 26 mega-ports in China and counting.

All those ports are structured under a variety of operational and financial structures but most with a significant participation of the State. In Cuba, the mega-port is an integrated concession where Odebrecht builds, and Singapore Authority operates while financing is shared by Brazil (85%), and Cuba (15%). In Jakarta, the Indonesia Port Corporation develops (three terminals and two fuel berths), then concessions by business unit. In Taiwan, the mega-port is fully state-funded. In Sri-Lanka, the Chinese build, finance, and own 85% of the project, the SRLA Port Authority finances and owns 15%, and the project does include a significant investment for breakwaters components (financed by a loan from the Asian Development Bank (ADB), of USD 300 million).

Some of the projects are greenfield such as Badagry/ Lagos Nigeria to be launched as main stream PPP, the two in Panama and the Qatar new port. Most have significant government participation, either in terms of ownership or financing, while some are fully privately financed (ATM in Lagos, Nigeria). The most common intervention by governments is the financing of "non-productive/non-direct revenue generating" port infrastructure and those components of the project are often undertaken as public works. The level of investment is considerable in most of those initiatives ranges from USD 500 million to USD 7 billion.

Figures 5.1 to 5.3 below illustrate the trends for the current and past decades in investments in ports around the world (based on IFC-International Financial Corporation and PPIAF- Public-Private Infrastructure Advisory Facility data base). Of note is the increasing share of greenfield (relative to brownfield) port projects, and the high incidence of port projects in East Asia, Latin America and South Asia, but with the Middle East catching up.

Figure 5.1. **Average annual private investment in seaports**
2000-2011 in low and middle-high income developing countries in billions USD

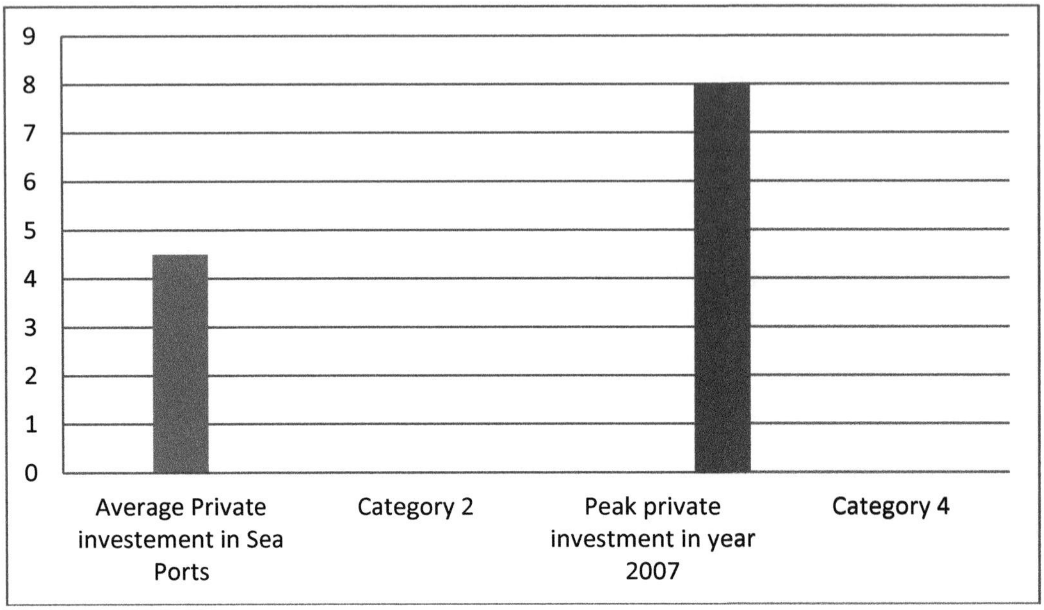

Source: IFC and PPIAF Data Base 2012.

Figure 5.2. **Private investment in seaport projects by region and modality**
2000-2012, billions USD

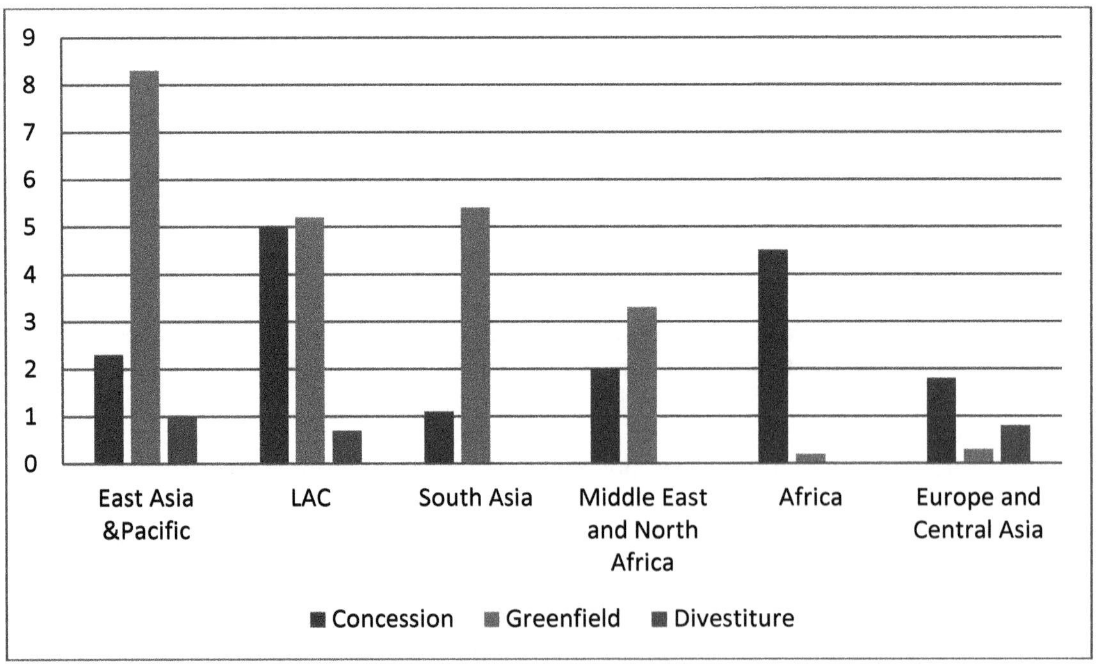

Source: IFC and PPIAF Data Base 2012.

Figure 5.3. **Percentage of greenfield and brownfield investments**
(in value terms) in two decades 1990-1999 and 2000-2011

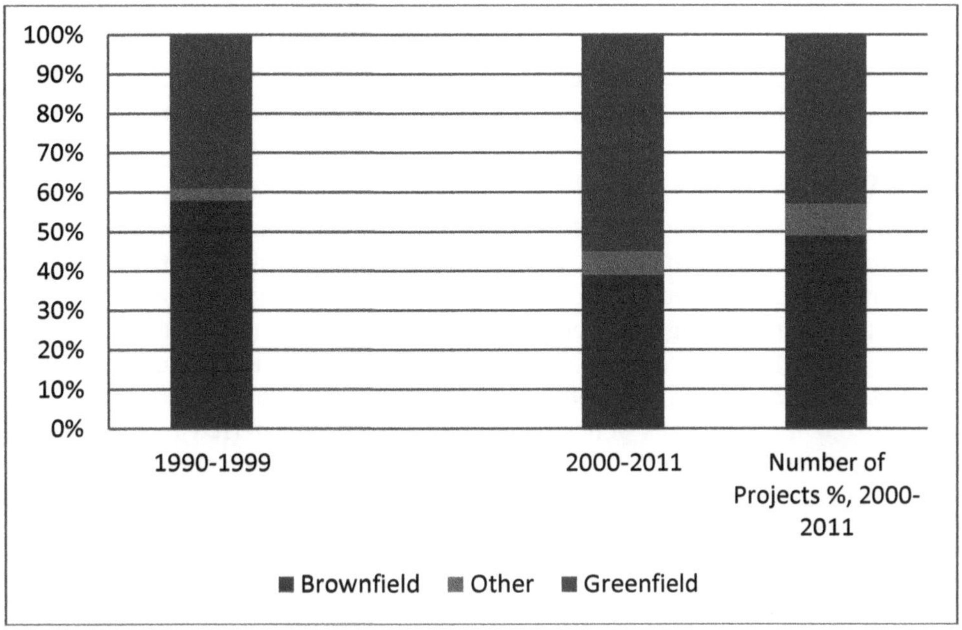

Source: IFC and PPIAF Data Base 2012.

Risk management in port concessions

As shown in Theys et al. (2010), one of the most critical issues in the development of a PPP contract is the identification and allocation of risks between the port authority and the private operators.

The huge dimension of some infrastructure projects (for instance ports) involves a number of potential risks. Depending on the definition, project risks can be decomposed to different groups. To facilitate discussion, one possible decomposition is presented below, as summarised in Table 5.1.

Table 5.1. **Types of risks associated to the development of an infrastructure**

Technical risk	Construction risk	Operating risk
Revenue risk	Financial risks	*Other risks*

Technical risks concern the engineering and project design failure (Grimsey and Lewis 2002). With regard to construction, the main risks are the possibilities of delays and cost overruns, as is also the case in other (transport) infrastructure projects. During the operating phase, the materialisation of operating risks leads to increased operating and maintenance costs. Usually the risks mentioned above are transferred to the private sector (depending on the cause) under the concession, PPP or privatisation mode, or retained with the government, with caveats, in the case of public works. We have not encountered research which would analyse or review the causes of individual types of risk in greater detail, specifically in the case of port infrastructure projects.

Revenue risks basically depend on the probability of changes in expected demand, due to overestimation or exogenous circumstances – for example, a demand reduction because a new competitive alternative to the port has become available or a major economic/financial crisis. Chile developed 3 risk mitigation mechanisms to make highway concession projects more attractive to bidders: Minimum Revenue Guarantee (MRG), Least Present Value of Revenues (LPVR) and Revenue Distribution Mechanisms (RDM). On the relationship between the operator of the infrastructure and its customers, Klein (1998) pointed out that the risks generally should not be transferred to the concessionaire if he cannot control or assess them more effectively than the customers. In general, demand is difficult to forecast, and transferring this risk to the private side is generally not considered to be a favourable option, especially in case strong competition between bidders is absent[4].

The materialisation of any one or several of the risks above contributes to the overall risk of project default (Grimsey and Lewis, 2002). In the context of the Chilean case, the revenue risk is a major one given the life span of the project, uncertain characteristics of the demand, and a number of external factors that can affect revenue. That risk is usually assigned to the private sector, with in some cases some sharing from the government through MRG. The other major risk on projects refers to construction, that encompasses cost overruns (on average 75% of projects in Latin America experience cost overruns and the mean of the cost overruns is about 35%)[5] and project delays (on average in Latin America, 65% of projects do experience significant delays in the six to 18 months range). For public works, those risks are usually allocated to the government with some caveats described in the tendering contract. In the case of concessions, PPP or privatisation that cost is usually borne by the private operator, again with some caveats depending on the underlying causes.

In summary, the main risks usually allocated to the private operator are (the stars illustrate the importance of individual risks):

- Revenue Risk ***** (high variance over predicted demand , and optimism bias much more common-realized revenues often much lower than predicts/expected demand)
- Construction Risk **** (about 75% of projects in Latin America experience cost overruns on average and the mean of cost overrun is about 35%).
- Technical Risk ***
- Financial Risk ***
- Operational Risk **
- Others risks (some possibly shared)

Considering the risk assessment, there is a wide range of techniques employed to assess them in mega-projects such as fault, event or decision tree analyses, Monte Carlo or sensitivity analysis, scenario planning, expected monetary or net present value, among others (Ebrahimnejad et al, 2010).

A proper risk allocation among public and private partners may be crucial in determining the success of the project. As such, it should be explicitly described and stated (the risk matrix and its allocation) in the contract design. The latter should detail the share of risks borne respectively by the public sector and the private partners, in a range covering from totally public from totally private. The stability or lack of adjustments to the stated risk allocation is indeed the crucial element of the contract to secure the expected benefits of the project. The core of renegotiations entails changes in the risk allocation matrix. Care should be therefore exercised in handling renegotiation requests. The dissuasion of inappropriate renegotiation demands is recommendable, because efforts and demands (by the private sector) to alter the risk allocation can be expected throughout the life of the project (the renegotiations conundrum). On average about 65% of PPP projects have been renegotiated in Latin America since 1990. Thus it is critical to credibly commit to respecting the sanctity of the contract. A high likelihood of contract renegotiations from one side or another may lead to opportunistic behaviour of both, further increasing the cost of finance and reducing the (public) benefit of projects to come.

The case of Chilean ports

Chilean international trade is served by 57 seaports, of which 25 are publicly used and only 10 are publicly owned, and are organized by the public agency *Empresa Portuaria Chilena (Emporchi)*, while 32 are privately used (Table 5.2).

Table 5.2. **Number of Ports in Chile**

Publicly used ports	**25**
Publicly owned	10
Privately owned	15
Privately used ports	**32**
Publicly owned	21
Privately owned	11
Total	**57**

According to Michea (2013), the reform of the port sector in Chile has been a successful experience expressed through financial results and a quality of service.

In 1978, seaports in Chile were characterized by the split of cargo handling between two different groups of workers. Specialised port workers performed stevedoring operations, while Emporchi employees did operations of loading/unloading. Both groups enjoyed some monopolistic positions. On the one hand, stevedores had strong limitations to the growth of their numbers, as each worker was required to have some special license *(matricula)* to be able to provide stevedoring services. This practice transformed stevedores into monopolists for those services, which resulted in high tariffs and low productivity. On the other hand, Emporchi was by definition a public monopoly, working at the state level and its workers constituted an important pressure group.

In 1980, the government decided to change the *status quo*. Legal changes were introduced in 1981 by passing a new Seaports' General Law, which effectively eliminated the monopoly of Emporchi in cargo loading operations, allowing private participation in those services. Almost simultaneously, a different law abolished the system of licenses for stevedoring, allowing any worker to perform those services for shipping companies. As compensation, the State made payments to the 2 700 workers that had lost their privileges and who were clearly opposed to any reform. These regulatory changes permitted the significant entry of new private operators and a competitive market for cargo handling was established. The impact on costs was substantial.

At the end of 1997, a law seeking to modernise State ports was passed, which sought to transform the Chilean port system and adapt it to the new needs of maritime transport. The law intended to introduce more private participation to achieve the objective of modernising the ports. The law envisaged splitting Emporchi into 10 autonomous public companies, which would run the 10 state ports, from Arica in the north to Punta Arenas in the south. These new companies will act as port authorities, managing ports' infrastructure, and are not allowed to provide cargo handling or berthing services.

The law also established that the new pier infrastructure had to be developed by private companies and through public tendering.[6] The idea was that the new port authorities should contract all these services with private operators, through licenses and concessions, including new pier infrastructure.

The "large scale port" in Chile

Description

The law of ports in Chile states that the Ministry of Transport and Telecommunications (MIT) is accountable for proposing "strategic plans": the MIT assumes the responsibility to coordinate plans for the long-term development of ports. Thus, the MIT is currently developing a national-scale port-planning instrument: the National Ports Development Plan (PNDP). One of the main proposals of this plan, according to its economic impact, is the *Puerto de Gran Escala* (PGE) to address the expected growth of trade and the limited capacity of exiting ports to service it in the next decade. The proposed location of the new PGE is in the middle of the country, and will service five of the most economically active country's Regions[7] (Michea 2013).

Currently Central Chile is served by two container terminals located in the Valparaíso Region, i.e. San Antonio and Valparaíso (depicted in Figure 5.4). The container transfer capacity currently available in the region is estimated 2.3 MM TEU/yr., which is distributed between:

- Terminal 1 in the Port of Valparaíso, operated by concessionaire TPS.
- Terminal 1 in the Port of San Antonio, operated by concessionaire STI.

The port authorities, *Empresa Portuaria San Antonio* (EPSA) and *Empresa Portuaria Valparaíso* (EPV), have successfully tendered their second container terminals recently. In 2011, EPSA awarded the 'Costanera-Espigón' project to *Puerto Central* concessionaire. In 2013, EPV gave the 'Terminal 2' concession to *OHL*.

The Puerto Central and Terminal 2 projects are expected to increase the installed capacity in slightly over 2 MM TEU/yr. All this capacity plus small increases, provided by minor infrastructure improvements to the existing terminals operated by TPS and STI should bring the total capacity in the area of influence to approximately 4.9 MM TEU/yr. by 2021.

Figure 5.4. **Existing container seaports in central Chile**

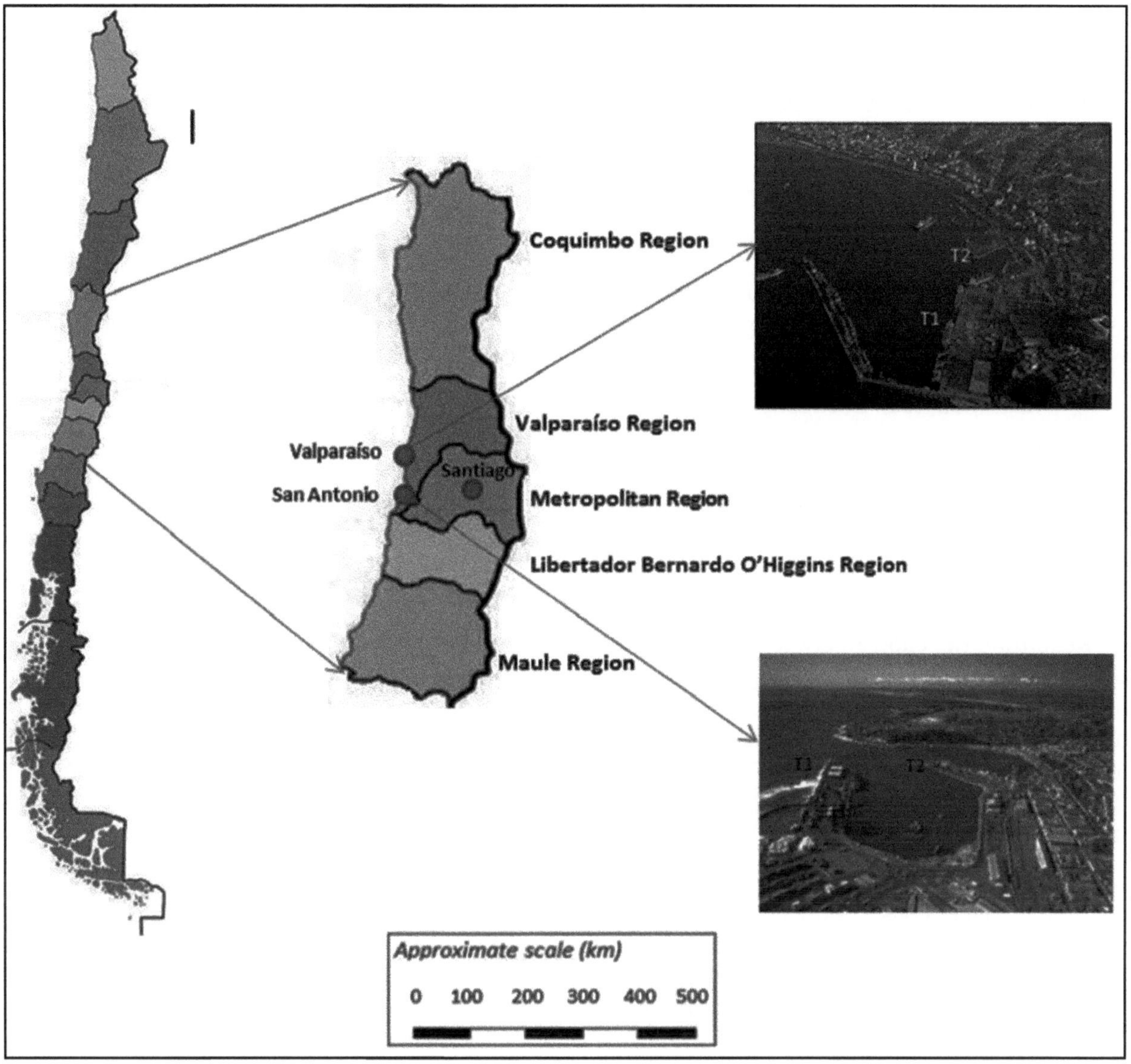

Source: Authors.

In terms of the demand forecasts, the total nominal capacity in the port system would be exhausted in 2025 by considering an average GDP growth of 4%, whilst at a rate of 5% this would occur in 2021. Therefore, the MIT concluded that at some point in the first half of the 2020s, demand growth in Central Chile would require an additional container capacity and it thus proposed the development of the PGE (Michea 2013).

For that purpose, in 2013 two alternatives are being considered: San Antonio and Valparaíso, as shown in Table 5.3.

Table 5.3. **Alternative locations and design specifications PGE**

San Antonio	Valparaíso
New capacity: 6 MM TEU/year	New capacity: 3 MM TEU/year
Estimated budget: USD 2 700 m.	Estimated budget: USD1 420 m.

Source: Michea (2013).

The proposal is to sequentially implement two mega-ports, one in each of those two locations. San Antonio might naturally support (at least) two port operators (terminals) given its technical specifications:

- maximum total dock length 3 560 m in two fronts,
- breakwater length 3 700 m,
- backup area: 170 ha, and
- nominal capacity: 6 MM TEU/yr.

The total investment is estimated at USD 2 750 million.

Valaparaíso with only one front would naturally support one port operator (although two could be considered, which would require splitting the terminal) as this is a natural setup, and given its technical specifications:

- maximum total dock length 1 770 m in one front,
- breakwater length 2 300 m,
- backup area 44 ha, and
- nominal capacity 3 MM TEU/yr.

In this case the total investment is estimated at USD 1 420 million.

Regarding the choice between the two identified locations it appears that from the logistics, extent of inducing competition, added capacity, cost basis (economies of scale) and back-up area standpoint, San Antonio might have an edge to be the first mover. This would be the case due to its apparently better intermodal links (in particular railroad), a larger capacity and backup area, and the ability to put in place at least two competing operators (two competing port terminals) and therefore a likely lower cost of services.

Introducing Private Participation in PGE and Financing Implications

One of the main issues here is to define a tendering model and financing implications for this large scale port. Concessions contracts are the dominant modes to introduce private participation in the port services. However, these very large and costly civil engineering works in building breakwaters for a port capable of handling 12,000 or 18,000 TEU ships could prove extremely costly and risky (unbankable) under current schemes. There are variants of the model that might make the project more bankable and attractive, while still generating the benefits sought by the government. In selecting the most appropriate structure for the tendering of the PGE, it is helpful to know what are the objectives of the design and implementation of the port's structure.

With regard to design and implementation, the objectives would be:

- securing the desired increased capacity,
- securing maximum competition in the provision of port services in the region,
- securing the lowest tariffs in port services (somehow linked to the previous objective),
- minimising the government's financial contribution or operational contribution, or quality in the provision of the services,
- reducing the transaction costs and delays in project implementation, government transfers, etc.

Generally speaking, the introduction of private participation is more feasible in already existing larger ports (landlord type) worldwide. In these ports the infrastructure can be split into separate terminals, which generates competition within the same port. Mostly, in these ports some services could be provided by private firms operating under licenses. In particular, for services that are easy to specify in a contract and do not involve the use of substantial elements of infrastructure. On the contrary, those private operators providing services that require the exclusive use of infra- or superstructure, must be subject to concession contracts, which stipulate under which conditions they can employ assets, and the obligations of the private contractors.

When considering private participation in the specific case of the PGE, the following points should be taken into account.

- Decision to separate the breakwaters component and if so, whether to tender them as public works or as concessions - Private Finance Initiative (PFI) or fee cost recovery.
- The first issue related to this option is whether there are any economies of scale or scope to be gained by bundling breakwater and port operations. In principle, if there are, they might not be too large since they are two very different types of activities and projects that require quite different sets of skills and know-how from the firms involved. In consequence, the number of potential firms that could be interested in a bundled project might be limited, constraining the benefits of competitive bidding. If unbundling of the tasks is selected, then the issue is whether the breakwaters projects should be undertaken as public works or as a concession/PPP. Our quick evaluation suggests that it would be reasonable to separate the breakwaters components from the rest of the port project.
- Another question to consider is whether there are complementary services-other port operations/services- to be added, assigned or/and provided by the breakwaters provider. If not, the sensible decision would be that the breakwaters be delivered as public works. From a value-for-money perspective, if there were any ancillary or related services beyond construction and maintenance (and it appears that that is not the case), the possibility of using a PPP/Concession or hybrid PFI[8] model could be considered.

Given the points stated above, three different schemes/options present themselves:

I. One single private operator and integrated concession.

This is the integrated concession model. In this case the private sector (one party) has to build and operate the whole port. The main advantage of this approach is to lower the transactional costs on tendering and coordination. Some of the disadvantages would be:

- A more complicated tendering process as it seems reasonable to assume a low number of tenders able to deal with the huge initial investment.
- A potentially excessive risk premium for the breakwater component, due to the probable inability of the concessionaire to price the construction risk.
- A more complicated financing structure.
- Tariffs alone are unlikely to support full cost recovery of investment.

This will result in i) some risk of monopoly power due to the duration of the concession (larger than usual due to the initial investment)[9]; and ii) the need of government financial support either directly (hybrid PFI) or through schemes like minimum revenue guarantees (MRG). Some other competition concerns such us the existence of collusion due to the low number of bidders can also to be taken into consideration.

II. Two or more private operators, several options.

Through this scheme, some of the previous risks could be diminished thanks to the split of the different services between different operators. Private firms operating under licenses or concession contracts could provide all of the port's services. One of the operators could build one part of the main infrastructure, recover costs as a PFI type project or through the other port operators paying fees for its use (either linked to traffic or set-up fixed monthly fee) or a hybrid.

The main characteristic in favour of this scheme is, that the market power could be better measured by the regulator. A negative aspect is that the transactional costs could be higher than in the previous model. The operator in charge of the construction would assume a huge initial investment, along with a less clear bankability of the project which depends on the type of cost recovery. It is likely that there would be a need for the financial support of the government for the breakwaters projects. However, at the same time it would lessen the need of a MRG.

A second possibility within this option is to separate the infrastructure component into two separate projects, one for the construction of the breakwaters and the other for the construction of the terminals. The latter then can be bundled with the terminal operations component or not. Here there a two further options. In the first there would be two infrastructure projects and private firms and a third component and firm for port operations. In the second there could just be two firms, one for the breakwaters construction and the other for the integrated port terminal construction and operations.

III. Public and private operators.

This refers to the landlord model, the most extensively used model worldwide for large ports, where the public sector builds and operates the infrastructure while the private sector runs all the port services and might finance or construct the residual infrastructure.

Two options could be considered in the Chilean case: i) the government builds all the infrastructure and then concessions the operations and services to the private sector; and ii) (if feasible) the government builds only the breakwaters infrastructure and then concessions the terminals and operations to the private sector. The main advantage is that the regulator could control the market power and the public sector would carry out the initial investment and then recover the fees from the operator and the shippers (or through taxes to facilitate bankability). The main disadvantage is the opportunity cost of the investment. If the breakwaters component could be separated from the port terminal component, the public sector would take care of the breakwaters component through traditional procurement. It could then could tender the remaining part of the project (integrated port terminal construction and port operations) to the private sector or even separate the task to be tendered to two separate firms.

This scheme also allows the creation of an independent company, from the combination of efforts of two or more entities in joint-ventures. The partnership between the public and the private sector would lead to recover the initial investment through cooperation.

It has to be noted that the different models commented above depend on the port law, which states that the new pier can only be developed by private firms. One question that might require a detailed interpretation of the law is whether the development/construction of breakwaters is also covered by the same law. The underlying concern is whether through the presence of a public good component or essential infrastructure, the law, and therefore the obligation that only the private sector can develop it, can be avoided. If such an interpretation is not possible, public participation in the construction of breakwaters might not be possible in Chilean ports, and all the negative aspects related to the absence of the public sector in the project would come into play.

As mentioned before, a possibility, if feasible, would be to split the construction (and tendering) of project works into two components. One component would entail the construction of breakwaters and the other the construction of port terminals (coastal side). That option is indeed quite feasible for the Valparaiso case. For the San Antonio case, although the option in principle is feasible, the port design makes this solution more difficult.

Table 5.4 below summarises the different alternatives models listed for the Chilean case.

Table 5.4. **Alternative models**

	Private Participation – One tender	Private Participation – 2 or more tenders	Public and –Private Participation
Pros	Lower transactional and coordination costs	Competition for the market (more bidders) and in the market	Risk allocation Public sector provides public services (breakwater)
Cons	Huge initial investment/financing issues Monopoly risk	A complex bidding process Higher transactional costs among operators Breakwater contract	Chilean law

Issues to Consider About the Most Desirable Structure and Financing for the PGE

Financial Model and Costing of the Breakwaters Component

It is crucial to have a cost estimation of the breakwaters component of the project and to have an idea of the financial model underlying the options discussed above. In particular it is necessary to estimate the tariff levels or revenue needed, as well as their impact on the demand and cost recovery patterns to assess the relations between all these elements. A simple value-for-money analysis might be useful to guide the discussion and to indicate the appropriate alternative.

Chilean Concession/PPP Law (Ports)

The Chilean Law establishes a general rule under which new pier infrastructure can only be developed by private companies and through public tendering. Nevertheless, the law does not mention new breakwater investments, which technically are but need not be piers. Another interpretation issue is that while the new pier infrastructure can only be developed by private companies, it remains unclear whether the government can pay for it in full or partially through a PFI model. It would appear so, but this should be confirmed. The questions therefore are: Can the government finance/undertake breakwaters investments? Can the government provide subsidies? Is there a need to modify the current Chilean concession model to include the public sector at the time to underwrite the risk and to finance the breakwater if that option proves to be the salient one?

A possible scheme could be based on the fact that the public sector assumes the development of the breakwater, due to the public service nature of the port, which would be recovered through taxes from different operators and user fees. The public sector should not expect private companies to assume the cost side of the infrastructure investment, because it does not allow them achieve an appropriate return (and tariff levels that might lead to full cost recovery appear to be unworkable, particularly given the natural uncertainties about the level of demand over the long life of the concession). There appears to be a consensus that the Law does not apply to essential public facilities as is the case for breakwaters, so the government could finance and undertake the breakwater component, if it chooses to do so. Indeed this point is of critical importance, because as long as the Chilean government wants to develop a large infrastructure projects like the PGE, its involvement in the funding of a part of this infrastructure (breakwaters) appears to be necessary.

The un-bundling of port and breakwaters projects/tasks and their allocation

Numerous issues arise when considering this option. Are there any economies of scale or scope to be gained by bundling breakwater and port operations? In principle, if there are, they might not be too large since they are two very different types of activities and projects that require quite different sets of skills and know-how from the firms involved. In consequence the number of potential firms that could be interested in a bundled project might be limited, reducing the benefits of competitive bidding. Another point to consider is whether other port services could be added, allocated or and provided by the breakwaters providers. If not, the salient decision would be to provide the breakwater components as public works. From a value-for-money perspective, if any ancillary or related services beyond construction and maintenance (and it appears that that is not the case) would exist, then the possibility of a PPP/Concession or hybrid PFI model could be considered. If the unbundling of the tasks is selected, then the question is whether the breakwater project should be executed as public works or as a concession/(PPP). Given all these considerations it appears that the prudent choice is to separate the breakwater component and let the government undertake it as a public works project.

Bankability of the Project and Level of Tariffs Needed for Cost/Investment Recovery

It is critical to assess the level of tariffs needed to support cost recovery and at the same time their relation with demand and competitive pressures. The financing, cost recovery, tariff levels and access fees need to be assessed, as well as any need for credit enhancement or other type of government support such as minimum revenue guarantees.

The required levels of revenue and tariffs can be roughly estimated, performing a simple financial exercise. Assuming identical cash flows every year, a 10% discount rate, a concession lifetime of 30 years and an initial investment of USD 14 200 million for Valparaíso and USD 2 700 million for San Antonio, the table below shows the revenue needs to make the project bankable and based on that the relevant tariffs.

Table 5.5. **Cash flows per project**

	Valparaíso	San Antonio
Investment	1 420 million USD	2 700 million USD
Traffic (TEUs)	3 million	6 million
N° Teus (round trip)	1.5 million	3 million
Cash Flow per TEU	USD 100.42	USD 95.47

Source: Authors calculations.

As the cash flows are defined as revenues minus costs, the numbers above should reflect the cash flows per TEU (revenue-price times quantity- less operating costs). Thus, the price per container is higher than 100.42 (Valparaíso) and 95.47 (San Antonio), respectively. Because the cost of operation is not included, the price will be higher, and the mark-up will evolve as a function of the operating costs. In addition, it should be noticed that the calculation assumes full operating capacity of the ports from day one, which will not be the case.

These numbers give additional support to the claim that the breakwater component should be implemented by the government to insure a better bankability of the PGE project.

Number of Operators

How many different operators are sufficient to enable a healthy degree of competition? While there is no universal rule, two or three operators (for the PGE terminals) might be enough to elicit a healthy degree of competition among them. Given the current number of 4 operators at the existing terminals at Valparaíso and San Antonio (albeit not PGE type), the competitive market could be substantially enhanced.

Eligibility to Participate in the Tendering of the New Port (terminals)

Should existing operators in San Antonio and Valparaíso be allowed to compete for the operation of the terminals at the new PGE? As long as there is more than one PGE operator (terminal), it does not seem necessary to disallow the current operators to participate in the tendering of the PGE terminals.

Award criteria

The common criteria could be the following:

- Awarder to the bid with the lowest composite transfer (tariff/fee) rate of required services (it will be the maximum tariff charged).
- LVP of revenues.
- Minimum Subsidy (or Largest Transfer). (The minimum subsidy the private partner would find acceptable to make the project bankable).
- Revenue Sharing (the share of the revenues the private partners are willing to share with the government.).

If compatible with a competitive environment, the standard LPV of revenues could fit the case. However, it would need to be aligned with potential risk mitigation or sharing from the government. In addition the criteria would be dependent on the project's structure and the related tendering procedures, i.e. are we tendering a single project or splitting it into various functions and firms. Minimum subsidies for components lacking full financial viability are a natural choice. Tariffs or transfers to government are often used as well but with very different distributional (equity) effects. The Chilean experience has shown that the current method of the integrated transfer/tariff has worked well in the past, so it might be a reasonable choice again.

Credit Enhancement and Government Assistance in the Financing to Make Projects Bankable

The possible options with private partners are:

- PFI model, full or partial (hybrid):

The private sector finances and operates while the government pays an annuity for the life of the concession and bears the demand risk.

- CRPAO[10]- payments for progress in Project's construction:

The private sector finances and operates the infrastructure and provides services while the government pays advances on the construction phase cost. For example, if 10 % of the project is completed, the government pays the equivalent amount (usually with a bond).

Additional instruments such as the Minimum Revenue Guarantees (MRG), bond issue with or without guarantees, an equity position and the issues, concerning refinancing and renegotiation also need to be taken into account.

Concluding remarks

As noted, the success of privatisations depends on how they are executed, to what terms and conditions and, especially, how they are regulated.

The introduction of the private sector in ports usually leads to improvements in their efficiency and productivity ratios. However, the privatisation processes per se (and the efficiency gains) do not directly imply better positions for all the agents involved in ports. Without a proper mechanism that enables an adequate economic regulation and considers all the involved parties, the results of the privatisation may fail to meet the expectations of the government.

Latin American experience provides evidence that, although port privatisations (or other forms of private participation) have led to reasonably favourable outcomes, the contracts may not have been well designed, the bids may have been aggressive, and the governments have failed to credible commit to a policy of no renegotiation and to uphold the sanctity of the bids, as is evident from the magnitude of renegotiations.

In future port concessions, the focus should be directed at auctions as is already the case in Chile. Governments and port agents should consider how to improve the performance of this mechanism by properly aggregating multiple criteria and should also consider the social dimension.

As shown in this paper, concessions are the usual way to introduce efficiency and competition in the port industry. The competition for the market is still the most common tool to reach the benefits of competition in the port industry Although the optimal way forward appears to be the introduction of competition between ports, which is indeed the case for Chile. The construction of mega-ports will introduce additional private operators, which will be forced to compete among themselves, thereby further strengthening competitive pressures (given the proximity of Valparaíso and San Antonio). The setup of a concession should always consider the competition to be its key objective when designing PPP port projects. However, he achievement of this objective has to be pursued with a high degree of transparency (Guasch, 2006).

This report discussed and presented a number of options in the design of the structure for the Chile Puerto de Gran Escala (PGE) project: division of project components, number of firms, public versus private roles and other aspects. How to select among the various options and move forward is the subject of future steps. In summary, it is of critical importance to identify the key objectives to be secured beyond the obviously desired increase in capacity. If the maximisation of competition were the overriding issue, it would appear that the San Antonio option with (at least) two terminal operators, and a third for the infrastructure component might be a salient one (as this the first project to be implemented). If the transaction costs and coordination issues are the key concerns, the best choice might be to award an integrated concession to a single party to benefit from the internalisation of many problems (integrated tariffs, costs allocations). If facilitating and ensuring financing is a critical factor, a PFI type arrangement (or the CRPAO model) for the infrastructure component with a separate concession for port terminal operations might be an option.

With regard to the discussion on the breakwaters components, given their different asset life cycle (50 years or more versus 30 years for port terminals), lack of complementarities (the breakwaters and the terminals involve two very different types of business and skills), and easier access to finance, it might be desirable to separate their construction from the terminals. In this case there are two options, the breakwaters works could be done by the government as a public works or as a concession and financed by access fees (if feasible) or as full or hybrid PFI. That choice will depend on the financial model and the extent of value for money. Of the two, the more reasonable choice appears to be a traditional procurement, where the public sector finances and tenders the works for the breakwater component. Taking the legal perspective into account, the current Chilean Law appears to allow such a choice.

In summary, regarding the structure of the project the best choice appears to be the third model presented here. In this model, the government takes upon itself to deliver the breakwater component and then tenders the terminals broken down in two parts (four could also be considered) using the current Chilean award criteria. Regarding eligibility, it would appear that as long as there are two or more PGE terminals to be tendered, the current operators of the Valparaíso and San Antonio could be allowed to participate in the tendering, without having to cancel their current concession. Finally, given the long gestation of the project, the long asset life-cycle and the natural uncertainties about the upcoming demand, the granting of an MRG might be unavoidable.

Regarding the choice among the two identified location options it would appear that from the logistics standpoint, San Antonio does have a significant edge and offers better value for money than Valparaíso. The reasons are its intermodal connections, in particularly railroad, greater capacity and the ability to foster more competition among operators. Our analysis thus points in the direction, that this should be the first project to be implemented.

Annex 1. **Tendering process**

International Bidding	
Bidder requirements	• Minimum Equity. • Qualified Operator.
Award criteria	• Minimum Average Tariff. • LPVR. • Criterion tiebreaker: maximum payment (validate value business).

Source: Araya Mena (2006).

Annex 2. **Concessions scheme**

Concession Contract	• Known ex-ante by bidders. • It is an instrument that contains all of the rights and obligations of the parties, including mechanisms for dispute resolution.
Concession Companies	• Governed by rules of public companies. • Consortium bidder must have at least 51% of the concessionaire. • Qualified Operator must own 35% of the concessionaire at least in the first five (5) years.
Object of Concession	• Development, maintenance and exploitation of the berthing front, including the provision of infrastructure, cargo handling and cargo storage.
Duration	• Between 15 and 20 years for the multipurpose terminals, extendable up to 30 years in case an investment into an expansion of the infrastructure is defined.
Labour Regime	• The concessionaire is free to hire its own employees. • Regime applicable: Labour Code.
Rates and Quality of Service Levels	• Public rates without arbitrary discrimination. • Rates for handling, loading and provision of infrastructure may not exceed the maximum weighted average fare offered. • Fees for other services: Tariff freedom. • Compliance with transfer speeds of minimum load to nave. • Compliance with transfer speeds of average load in four (4) previous quarters (Not applicable in the case of Arica). • Compliance with timeouts.
Rules to limit exercise of dominant position: established by the antitrust commission and reviewable after a certain period (5 years)	• Shareholdings in companies awarded other concessionaires in state ports or privately operated ports in the same region subject to maximum levels (restriction on horizontal integration). • Shareholding in concessionaire serving "relevant users" in other activities is subject to maximum levels (restriction vertical integration).
Mandatory initial investment	• First Stage: Not contemplated. • Later stages: Terminal in each case and terminal for the shipment of bulk minerals in the case of Antofagasta and Arica.
Obligations of the port companies to the State	• Provision of common public goods and general administration of the port, including terminals not concessioned. • Minimum rates for the services for the provision of infrastructure and cargo storage: Not lower than those registered by the operator with maximum upper limit. • Maximum fare, applicable to the service provision of common goods (port user charge). • Tender of new fronts of berth. • The only economic factor for the award and use will be the amount of money offered. • Port companies retain the right to bid and/or grant the right to operate other fronts of berth of the port.
Labour Aspects	• Programs of forced lay-offs for workers under state owned ports/operations. • Workers of the Empresa Portuaria de Chile. • Worker service providers to private stevedoring companies, without a contract or relationship with the company.

Source: Araya Mena (2006).

Figure 5.5. **Existing container seaports in central Chile**

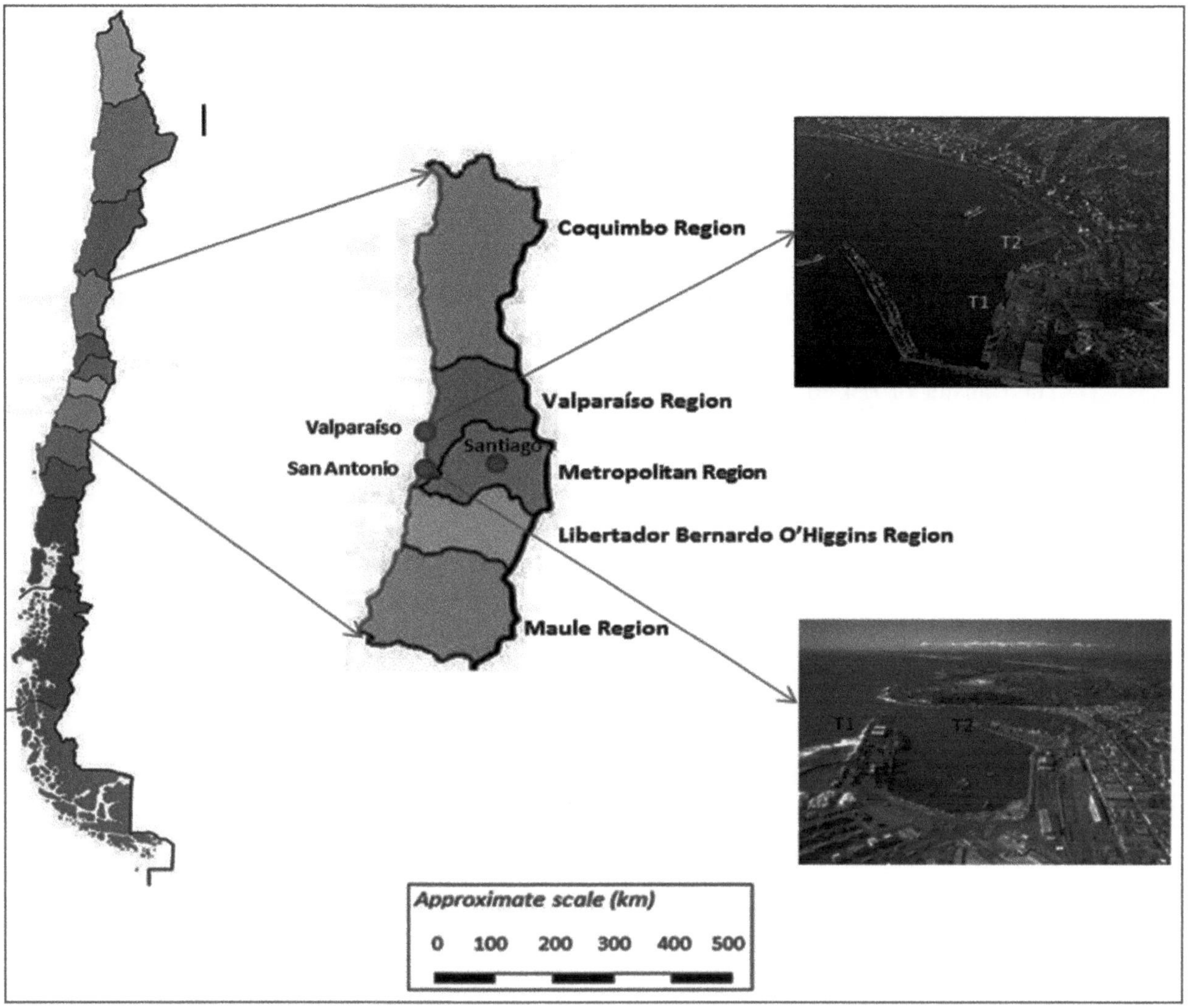

Notes

1. See Trujillo and Nombela (2001) for extension of this issue.
2. In the sense, that the professional capacity of the economic regulator cannot be developed over night.
3. Theys et al (2010) provides a description of recent issues emerging in the awarding process.
4. The transfer of risk to the private side does not mean it is dissolved, but that the private sector calculates a premium for accepting that risk. Because information asymmetry is present, the premium might be disproportionate to the actual risk if there is no competition to reduce it to an efficient level. The consequences are less favourable bids or substantially higher cost of financing, respectively.
5. It should be noted, that this is a crude assessment of cost overruns, as it involves traditional and PPP projects alike, with contract value as reference estimate and is therefore not comparable with academic studies, which deal exclusively with the magnitude and sources of cost overruns (and benefit shortfall) and consider the two types of procurement strictly separately. But the incidence and level of cost overruns is significantly higher in traditional public works than on PPP (Guasch 2006)
6. Annex 1 and 2 provides more-detailed information on tendering and contracting procedures in Chile.
7. The regions of Coquimbo, Valparaíso, O'Higgins, Maule, and Metropolitana of Santiago.
8. For example a model in which the government participates with its own equity, but where the private sector still retains the majority ownership or the project company/port.
9. This could be potentially mitigated by the existence of the two neighbouring ports of Valparaíso and San Antonio, but nevertheless it will end with a quasi-capture of demand as the new generation large ships is unable to dock at these ports. However here again a possible mitigation effect could play through the developments of the (forthcoming) port of El Callao/San Lorenzo in Peru.
10. *Certificados de Reconocimiento de Derechos del Pago Annual por Obra*s - Certificates Acknowledging the Right to Collect the Annual Construction Payment.

References

Andres, L., Guasch, J.L., Diop, M., 2007, Un balance de las privatizaciones en el sector infrastructura, Nueva Sociedad, 207.

Araya Mena, 2006, La Estructura de las Concesiones en Puertos en Chile, Mimeo.

Baird, A., Valentine, V., 2007 in Brooks, M., Cullinane, K.P.B. (Eds.) Devolution, Port Governance and Port Performance, Research in Transportation Economics, Volume 17.

Barja, G., McKenzie, D., Urquiola, M., 2004. Capitalization and Privatisation in Bolivia: An Approximation to an Evaluation. Center for Global Development Conference on Privatisation and Income Distribution, February.

Brooks, M.R., 2004. The governance structure of ports. Review of Network Economics, 3 (2).

Crampes, C., Estache, A., 1998. Regulatory trade-offs in the design of concession contracts. Utilities Policy, 7 (1), pp. 1-13.

Culliane, K.B.P., Song, D.W., 2002. Port privatisation policy and practice. Transport Reviews, 22 (1), pp. 55-75.

Delfino, J.A., Casarin, A., 2003. The Reform of the Utilities Sector in Argentina. In Ugaz, C. and C. Waddams Price, ed.

Engel, E, Fisher, R., Galetovic, A., 2000. The Chilean Infrastructure Concessions Program: Evaluation, Lessons and Prospects for the Future, (with R. Fischer and A. Galetovic), in Spanish, in F. Larraín and R. Vergara (eds), The Economic Transformation of Chile, Santiago: CEP, 201–246, 2000.

Ennis, H., Pinto, S., 2003. Privatisation and Income Distribution in Argentina. Center for Global Development Conference on Privatisation and Income Distribution, February.

Estache, A., Guasch, J.L., Iimi, A., Trujillo, L., 2009. Multidimensionality and renegotiation: evidence from transport sector public-private-partnership transactions in Latin America. Review of Industrial Organization, 35, pp. 41-71.

Estache, A., Trujillo, L., 2004. La privatización en America Latina en la década de los años 90: Aciertos y errores. Revista Asturiana de Economía, 31.

Estache, A., Guasch, J.L., Trujillo, L., 2003. Price caps, efficiency payoffs and Infrastructure Contract Renegotiation in Latin America.World Bank Policy Research Working Paper No. 3129.

Estache, A.; Rossi, M. A. 2010. Regulatory Agencies: Impact on Firm Performance and Social Welfare Policy Research Working Paper 4509. World Bank. CCRP Discussion-Paper-22-Stern-March_13

Gassner, K.; Popov, A.; Pushak, N. 2009. Does Private Sector Participation Improve Performance in Electricity and Water Distribution? Trends and Policy Options; no. 6. The World Bank. González, M.M. and Trujillo L. 2009. "Efficiency Measurement in the Port Industry: A Survey of Empirical Evidence" Journal of Transport Economic and Policy 43(2): 157-192.

Guasch, J.L., Laffont, J.J., Straub, S., 2008. Renegotiation of concession contracts in Latin America. Evidence from the water and transport sectors. International Journal of Industrial Organization, 26, pp. 421-442.

Guasch, J.L., 2006. Rethinking Private Sector Participation in Infrastructure: Towards effective Public Private Partnership-Concessions in the Provision of Infrastructure Services. Report no. 32674-PE. World Bank Institute, Washington, D.C.

Guasch, J.L., 2004. Granting and Renegotiating Infrastructure Concessions. Doing it right. World Bank Institute, Washington, D.C.

Guasch, J. L., 2003. Concessions: Bust or Boom? An Empirical Analysis of Fifteen Years of Experience in Concessions in Latin America and Caribbean, The World Bank Institute, Washington DC.

Hoffman, J., 2001. Latin American Ports: Results and Determinants of Private Sector Participation. International Journal of Maritime Economics, 2001, 3, pp. 221-241.

Inter-American Development Bank (2002) The privatisation Paradox, Latin American Economic Policies, 18.

Juhel, M.H., 2001. Globalization, Privatisation and Restructuring of Ports. International Journal of Maritime Economics, 3 (2), pp. 139-174.

Michea (2013). Iniciativa de Puerto de Gran Escala en Chile. Ministerio de Transporte, Santiago, Chile.

Mueller, B., 2001. Institutions for commitment in the Brazilian regulatory system, Quarterly Review of Economics and Finance, V. 41, 5, 621-643.

Paredes, R., 2003. Redistributive impact of privatisation and regulation in utilities in Chile. In Ugaz, C. and C. Waddams Price, ed.

Resende, M., Facanha, L.O., 2002. Privatisation and efficiency in Brazilian telecommunications: an empirical study. Applied Economic Letters, 9, 823-826.

Saundry, R., Turnbull, P.,1997. Private profit, public loss: The financial and economic performance of U.K. ports. Maritime Policy and Management, 24(4), 319–334.

Thompson, L.S. and Budin, K. J., 1997. Global Trend to Railway Concessions Delivering Positive Results, Public Policy for the Private Sector", Note No.134, December, World Bank, Washington.

Torero, M, Pasco-Font, A., 2003. The social impact of privatisation and regulation of utilities in Peru. In Ugaz, C. and C. Waddams Price, ed.

Trujillo, L. and Gonzalez, M., 2011. Maritime ports. In M. Finger and R. Künneke (ed.) International Handbook for the Liberalization of Infrastructure. Edward Elgar.

Trujillo, L. and Nombela, G., 2000. Seaports. In Estache, A. and De Rus, G. (eds.) Privatisation and Regulation in Transport Infrastructure: Guidelines for Policymakers and Regulators, WBI Development Studies, Banco Mundial, Washington DC.

List of participants

Mary R. BROOKS — Chair
Adjunct Professor
Rowe School of Business
Dalhousie University
PO BOX 15000
Halifax, NS, B3H 4R2 Canada

Gordon WILMSMEIER — Rapporteur
Economic Commission for Latin America and the Caribbean (ECLAC)
Natural Resources and Infrastructure Division (NRID)
Infrastructure Services Unit (ISU)
Santiago
Chile

Michele ACCIARO — Rapporteur
Assistant Professor of Maritime Logistics
Kühne Logistics University (KLU) -
Wissenschaftliche Hochschule für Logistik und Unternehmensführung
Großer Grasbrook 17
20457 Hamburg
Germany

Luis GUASCH — Rapporteur
Corresponding author Professor of Economics
University of California San Diego
Senior Policy Advisor
The Growth Dialogue
George Washington University
Washington DC
USA

Gabriel ALDONEY VARGAS
Consultant
Chile

Patricio ARRAU PONS
Presidente
Gerens Capital
Padre Mariano 272, Piso 2
Providencia
Santiago
Chile

Alberto CAMARERO ORIVE
Director del Departamento de Ingeniería Civil.Transportes
Escuela de Ingenieros de Caminos, Canales y Puertos
Universidad Politécnica de Madrid
c/ Profesor Aranguren s/n
28040 Madrid
Spain

Carlos CANAMERO
Chemin de la Cretaux 25
CH-1196 Gland
Switzerland

Ronald FISCHER
Centro de Economía Aplicada,
Departamento de Ingeniería Industrial
CEA-DII, Universidad de Chile
República 701
Santiago
Chile

Stephen S FITZROY
Senior Vice President
Economic Development Research Group, Inc.
155 Federal Street
Suite 600
Boston, MA 02110
USA

Graham FRASER
Director
Focus Maritime (North West) Limited
3TL Waterloo Warehouse
Trafalgar Dock
Waterloo Road
Liverpool
L2 0BH
United Kingdom

Franco GANDOLFO
Development & Business Manager
Valparaíso Port Authority
Av. Errazuriz 25
Valaparaiso
Chile

Joseph HINEY
Irish Research Council Government of Ireland Postgraduate Scholar
School of Law and Government
Dublin City University
Director Drogheda Port Company
Ireland

Gloria HUTT
Undersecretary of Transport
Ministerio de Transportes y Telecomunicaciones
Amunategui 139, piso 7
Santiago
Chile

Harald JAEGER
CEO
Valparaíso Port Authority
Av. Errazuriz 25
Valaparaiso
Chile

Juan Marcos MANCILLA
Jefe de Desrrollo y Estudios
Valparaíso Port Authority
Av. Errazuriz 25
Valaparaiso
Chile

Andreas MEYER
(former General Manager for the Hamburg-Sued Group in Argentina, Paraguay, Uruguay)
Consultant
AMCLogistics
Argentina

Alexis MICHEA
Ministry of Transport
Ministerio de Transportes y Telecomunicaciones
Amunategui 139, piso 7
Santiago
Chile

Rodrigo MONSALVE RIQUELME
Gerente General
Portuaria TSV
Avda. Blanco Encalada 547.
Talcahuano
Chile

Vincent POIRIER-GARNEAU
APOYO Consultoría
Av Armendáriz 424
Lima, 18
Peru

Athanasios PALLIS
Dept of Shipping, Trade & Transport
University of the Aegean
2 Korai St
82 100 Chios
Greece

Ganesan RAGHURAM
Indian Institute of Management
Ahmedabad
India

Andrés RENGIFO BRICEÑO
Antonio Bellet 444 Of 203
Providencia
7500032 Santiago de Chile
Chile

Aldo SIGNORELLI
CEO, San Antonio Port Authority
Alan Macowan 0245
San Antonio
Chile

Dong-Wook SONG
Professor of Transport and Logistics
Transport Research Institute
Edinburgh Napier University
Merchiston Campus
Edinburgh EH10 5DT
United Kingdom

Beatriz TOVAR DE LA FÉ
Titular de Universidad
Departamento de Análisis Económico Aplicado
University of Las Palmas de Gran Canarias
Las Palmas de Gran Canaria
Spain

International Transport Forum Secretariat

Mr. Stephen PERKINS, Head of Research